praise for Surf Like a Girl

"This book will get you stoked. A must-read."

—KATHY ZUCKERMAN, the original inspiration for the character Gidget

"*Surf Like a Girl* should be required reading for any girl
who ever thought about picking up a surfboard.
If you surf every day, just took one lesson,
or are still fantasizing about your first session,
this book will help you do so much more confidently.
Even I learned something new!"

—HOLLY BECK, professional surfer and IWS president

"Rebecca Heller is like your big sister;
she has already made all the important mistakes so readers don't
have to make them all over again. Plus, it's a fun read!"

—ALANA BRENNAN, professional surfer

"Wow! A fun and flower-friendly way to explain
everything a girl should know about surfing!"

—ELISE GARRIGUE, surfer for Rip Curl

"*Surf Like a Girl* is funny, smart, and packed with information.
Even though I've been surfing for years, I found so much
I could relate to. This book is super sick!"

—MELANIE BARTELS, professional surfer

Surf Like a Girl

Surfing with Aloha

The Surfer Girl's Ultimate Guide to Paddling Out, Catching a Wave, and

Rebecca Heller

Illustrations by Sujean Rim

THREE RIVERS PRESS
NEW YORK

Published in the United States by Three Rivers Press, an imprint of the
Crown Publishing Group, a division of Random House, Inc., New York.
www.crownpublishing.com

THREE RIVERS PRESS and the Tugboat design are registered trademarks of
Random House, Inc.

Library of Congress Cataloging-in-Publication Data is available upon request

ISBN 1-4000-8272-2

Printed in the United States of America

Design by Maggie Hinders

10 9 8 7 6 5 4 3 2 1

First Edition

All things considered—maybe I was just a woman in love with a surfboard.

—FROM *GIDGET*, BY FREDERICK KOHNER

Contents

Foreword

BY ROCHELLE BALLARD

THE LOVE I HAVE FOR THE OCEAN was in me since I first learned to walk. I grew up on Kauai, and I was always in the water. When I was eleven years old, my dad initiated me into surfing. It was really scary when I first started. I had a lot of confidence in the water, and all I wanted was to surf—until it was time to paddle out. When it came down to it, I was afraid of surfing. I don't know why. It must have been the power of the ocean and the feeling that as much as I wanted to, I had no idea what I was doing.

I started off on a soft board. It was old and heavy, and I would always pearl on the takeoff. I also kept getting a rash from the raw foam unravelling on the board. For a while, I was close to quitting out of pure frustration. Then a friend of mine took me out to a wave that was a soft, long pealing point break over a shallow reef. I told him how frustrated I was getting on my soft board, so he traded boards with me out in the lineup and said to try his out. It was a beautiful fiberglass board with the coolest airbrush artwork. I climbed up onto the board and paddled for a wave. It glided through the water as I stroked into a really nice-looking two-foot wall. I stood up and turned the board toward the open face and started weaving down the line. I was so excited—I must have had the biggest grin on my face. I rode it all the way to the inside until the wave finally stopped breaking. I paddled out as fast as I could to catch another one. At that moment, I knew I was hooked for life. When I got home, I told my parents about it and asked for a board just like that one. Sure enough, I got one that Christmas (with the airbrush and everything).

From that point on, I surfed with the boys. Back then, there weren't too many surfer girls. I was such a little tomboy, that even if there were other girls out, I probably still would have surfed and hung out with the boys. Being around the boys was challenging and they pushed my surfing, but most of all I had lots of fun with them. Plus, the boys were cute and had muscles.

When I was in high school, my girlfriends and I would go to the beach, lie on the shore, and check out the boys. I could only lay there for so long, then I'd have to grab my surfboard and paddle out. My girlfriends would get irritated with me, because they'd get sunburnt and tired of waiting for me while I was out surfing. I wished they surfed, too, and that we could have fun catching waves instead of just lying on the beach. They always wondered why I surfed so much.

I've been surfing for twenty-one years now, and I'm more surf-stoked now than I was as a grom. Just this last week, I surfed all day every day, and I scored some really sick waves! It was sheet glass, not a cloud in the sky. The waves rose from 2 to 3 feet gradually through the week, increasing up to 8 to 10 feet in size, and stayed sunny and glassy the whole time. That's what you call an epic swell.

Surfing is definitely a natural addiction. Once you get hooked, it sucks you into a world that is challenging, fun, exciting, adventurous, and beautiful. Surfing is art in motion—liquid energy surrounding you from head to toe. A surfer has the ability to ride that energy, and with enough practice, tunes in to it and finds its rhythm.

I'm now on my thirteenth year on the ASP world championship tour and in the running for a world title. I've traveled the world many times and surfed some of the best waves on the planet. I've won prestigious contests, been in the movies, and made lots of other exciting accomplishments. I enjoy just about every kind of wave and condition the ocean has to offer. Through everything, I've found that overcoming fear—the kind of fear I felt way back when I was first learning to surf, and the kind of fear I encounter during high-performance surfing and on big waves—is always a learning experience. One step at a time, one challenge at a time, and enjoying every minute of it is what makes life so great.

When I picked up *Surf Like a Girl,* I thought, Do girls really need a surf guide geared specifically toward them? Why does women's surfing need to be spelled out? Why do women need a book that tells us how to surf and how to change in the parking lot? I kept thinking that you have to earn the title of surfer by getting out there and working at it, until you have it down. It shouldn't just be handed to you because you own a pair of board shorts.

But I read the book straight through, and I thought about the girl who doesn't have anyone to teach her how to surf and feel comfortable in the ocean. I thought, What if this girl had never stepped foot in the ocean but had a deep desire to surf or was inspired by surfing? That made me realize the value of this book and the impact that it can make on someone who otherwise wouldn't get a peek into that world.

Surf Like a Girl can guide and inspire girls. It has everything you want to know to get you started and educated about the sport—and it's fun to read. The history chapter in particular is really valuable, because being aware of how far women have come is something that has always been important to me. It's my hope that every hot up-and-coming surfer knows about Rell Sunn and Joyce Hoffman and the other major surfers who have been big inspirations to all of us.

In the mid-1990s, the women's surf clothing boom media frenzy had reporters asking why is women's surfing such a big trend, how long it would last, and what's the difference between men's surfing and women's surfing? At the beginning, these questions made total sense to me. But I think it's pretty amazing that, now, it's all these years later and they're still asking the same questions. I always say that women surfers are here to stay, and I try to remind people that women have been surfing since the beginning of the sport—whether or not the majority of the population knew it! Women surfers have been discriminated against and have overcome more challenges than men to be where they are today. They've juggled the balancing act of being tomboys who love the adventure of changing on the side of the road, taking on waves that scare the crap out of them, and hanging with the boys, all the while possessing femininity, poise, grace, domestic instincts, and the ability to give birth and mother a child. I know that one day soon people will stop seeing women surfers as a trend and instead see them as an inherent part of surf culture. My best girlfriends and I all go out and surf together. We have tons of fun and are inspired by one another's abilities. It's great to see more girls surfing and having a good time.

Today, both men and women are pushing surfing beyond a level ever thought possible. How cool is that? That's where it should lie. The fact is that both men and women have broken down barriers and taken on the impossible and made it possible.

So, I say don't surf like a girl or like a guy. Surf like you. Take on all the challenges that surfing has to offer and enjoy every minute of it.

Introduction

WHETHER YOU ARE JUST NOW READY TO START SURFING or you have been surfing for years, this book is for you, surfer girl. There are more women out in the water than ever before. We are no longer content to sit on the beach just watching our boyfriends. With movies like *Blue Crush,* clothing lines like Roxy, and the resurgence of the longboard, it is no wonder why. Girls with surfboards are in movies, on the pages of magazines, and on TV. They have their own shows, their own sponsors, their own clothes. But it's not just an image. At almost every spot these days there are at least a handful of girls out in the water, and some are shredding harder than the guys. It isn't enough for us just to be spectators anymore. We girls go out there and do it!

Why are so many girls hitting the water? Maybe for the same reasons you picked up this book. Were you inspired by Anne Marie from *Blue Crush;* the girls of MTV's *Surf Girls;* or Holly Beck, Chelsea Georgeson, and Veronica Kay from *Boarding House: North Shore?* Did you see a girl in a magazine or on a commercial and think, *I can do that?* Have you watched friends or boyfriends going out and you're tired of being left behind? Whatever reason gets you started, the actual sport of surfing is what is going to get you hooked.

But why surfing? What makes it so darn appealing? Is it harnessing the power of the ocean or being at one with it? Is it taking on the guys or checking them out? Because it looks cool? Because our friends are doing it? Different people have different reasons, but what I know is that when you are surfing, you feel like you are flying; you feel a part of nature, and it feeds your soul. Surfers get a bad rap because when they talk about surfing, their eyes glaze over and they slip into some other part of their brain that seems to be a little sunbaked; but really, we are just thinking about our last ride—or our next one. You might think we're taking it all a little too seriously, but it happened to me and I can see it in other people's eyes: once you stand up on your first wave, you're done for. All you can think about is the next time you are going to get out in the water. You start getting up and going to bed early. You spend all your time at the beach. You've got "surf stoke." It's the best kind of drug there is: it's free and it has no harmful side effects.

What's great about surfing is that you don't need to be a professional or a team member to participate. There's no competition. It's just you and your board and the water. Man (or woman!) versus nature. All you have to do is look to yourself to make it as challenging or as much plain fun as you want it to be. The person having the most fun is always the winner, whether she can stand up or not.

While surfing is an individual sport, it is also a super social activity. Small summer waves and good weather leave you lots of time to chat it up out in the water. Going out with a crew is the most fun; encouraging each other and pushing each other to improve is what makes surfing with friends such a blast. Even if you don't have a group to go out with, you will start to recognize people at your local break, where you will certainly develop feelings of camaraderie. And being a girl in the water has its benefits. Girls, as opposed to our more macho counterparts, are actually out there to have fun. There is often a group of stunned guys trying to look tough and hoard waves as girls socialize with their friends and cheer each other on.

The sport of surfing is only half of it. Check out our playground! You might surf reef breaks where bright blue and yellow fish come in and out of focus as the ocean ebbs and flows or beach breaks where dolphins (which you could swear were trained at Sea World) jump and dive in the waves. There is something that feels so right about floating over a rhythmic sea. Something peaceful. Getting tumbled is only Mother Nature's awesome power reminding you that while she may let you charm her, she can certainly never be conquered.

Surfing is not easy. You can't just pick up a board and head out and hope to rip it up out in the water. Just like other sports, it takes a lot of practice to become skilled. What might make surfing harder than most other sports is that your playing field is a constantly changing canvas. Surfing blends a rare combination of athleticism and grace that is usually required of figure skaters and ballerinas. Watching great surfers (professional or soul) is like watching a distilled dance of human and water, a person at one with the ocean. Catching the perfect wave—being in just the right spot at just the right moment and taking the ride—feels like hitting a hole in one or a home run. One moment of sheer perfection. And even when your arms are weary, you paddle back out in hope of catching another.

So what does *Surf Like a Girl* offer you? Well, it's not exactly a how-to book. It doesn't intend to teach you to surf (you can only do that by getting out in the water!), but it gives beginners the help they need to get started and offers enough information for the girl who's been surfing for years.

What to wear? Where to go? What's the difference between a long-board and a shortboard? When it comes to these issues, *Surf Like a Girl* will set you straight. And it will get into all the girly stuff, such as the best way to wear your hair and how to preserve your pedicure from surfing's impact. Hey, these are important issues!

This book is also for the landlocked girl who is a surfer in spirit, because you don't always need waves to be a surfer girl. All you need is the right attitude! When the waves are miles away, *Surf Like a Girl* will help you keep your surfing cool by suggesting inland activities and lifestyle tips that will make you a surfer girl wherever you are.

As a surfer girl, you will need wave knowledge and ocean smarts to conquer different conditions. And there are rules and etiquette just as there are for any other sport. Even though some of the rules and practices are unspoken, they are really important. No question is ever stupid, but sometimes directing one to the hot guy you are trying to get a date with can be slightly embarrassing. Enter *Surf Like a Girl*—everything you need to know but were afraid to ask. This book intends to answer all the "detail" questions that boys would never ask and men could never answer.

I hope this book will inspire you to get out there and be the best surfer you can be. Every girl can be a surfer girl, and by that I mean a girl who is courageous and brave, independent and fun. You don't need to be able to stand up on a board to be a surfer girl. You just need to be the girl who goes out there and does whatever she sets her mind to.

Why do we surf? You will have to answer that question for yourself, but I'll tell you, a parking lot filled with gorgeous guys changing under their towels doesn't hurt.

CHAPTER I

Getting Started

S O YOU WANT TO BECOME A SURFER? Right on. Here are the essentials to help you get started.

What to Wear: Be a Surfer Girl from the Inside Out

What surfers wear depends on the temperature of the water. In tropical climates you may see surfers in nothing but bathing suits. Some surfers will cover up with rash guards and board shorts to protect their skin and swimsuits from the sun and board rash. Wet suits in varying degrees of warmth are worn as the water temps dip.

SUNSCREEN

Start with generous amounts of sunscreen. According to dermatologists, a sun protection factor (SPF) of 15 doesn't cut it anymore. Use waterproof sunscreens with an SPF of 45 or higher with UVA and UVB protection. Be sure to apply liberally at least twenty minutes before you go out in the sun and reapply it every hour or two. (Wear sunscreen not only when you are surfing, but also anytime you are out playing in the sun, even on overcast days.) Sun can damage your skin and cause premature aging and wrinkles—ew! Or worse, it can cause skin cancer. While you may want to look twenty-one at seventeen, you don't want to look forty at twenty-five!

BATHING SUIT

Wear a comfortable and secure bathing suit. The ocean can throw you around as if you're in a washing machine, so skimpy tops and loose bottoms can come off in a hurry. Getting "worked" is embarrassing enough. Coming up exposed would only add insult to injury. When you're as good as, say, Rochelle Ballard, you can think about wearing a sexy bikini when you paddle out, but trust me, until then, look for athletic swim suits, such as full pieces, tank suits, and boy-cut shorts. Remember you are going to be doing athletic activities  when you surf, so make sure your 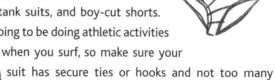 suit has secure ties or hooks and not too many extras, like bows or beads, that could rub or catch on your board. Choosing a stylish suit is fine. Just make sure it fits properly so it doesn't give the boys a peek. Also, it's a good idea to look for suits with a UPF (ultraviolet protection factor) of 50 or higher.

RASH GUARD

I strongly suggest wearing a rash guard over your bathing suit. A rash guard is either a long- or short-sleeved shirt made mainly of Lycra that does what its name implies. Rubbing against the wax on your board can leave little red bumps on your perfect skin, or it can pull at the fabric of your suit. A rash guard worn over your swimsuit will protect your skin from board rash and keep your suit looking new, as well as protect you from being exposed when a rough wave threatens to separate you from your bathing suit. Worn under a wet suit, a rash guard protects you from wet-suit seams that may irritate your skin. And a rash guard with UPF will further protect your skin from the sun. Rash guards cost a little more than a regular shirt, from $30 to $50, but they are well worth the price! You can pick one up at any surf shop. If you don't have a rash guard, a tight-fitting cotton T-shirt will do a similar job, but it will retain more water and it won't dry out as quickly.

HINT Board rash is a common condition. Exposed skin rubbing against your board and wax when you are getting up and lying down can cause your skin to become red and raw (most often on your thighs, stomach, and inner arm), and you may get little red bumps or cuts. Wet suits, rash guards, and board shorts will protect you from board rash.

BOARD SHORTS

Like rash guards, board shorts protect your skin from rashes and the sun and keep your bathing suit in good shape. And they are a great addition to the surfer girl's wardrobe! Since they're multifunctional, you can wear them around town, to the beach, or in the water. Board shorts look like regular shorts except that they are made of a synthetic superfast-drying material (usually polyester), so they are lightweight and durable. Knee-length board shorts offer a little more protection from rashes and the sun than the shorter version, but the choice is up to you. Board shorts can be found at surf shops and beyond (you can probably find them in your local department store). They run about the same price as rash guards. Make sure to look for shorts with Velcro and/or lace ups, since you will be lying on your stomach while paddling. You don't want lumpy buttons nagging at you while you're surfing (and if they're metal, they might rust).

WET SUIT

Most of the year, however, you will be donning a wet suit. Snug-fitting wet suits prevent heat loss as your body warms the water that seeps into the suit. Wet suits are essential as the water cools in nonsummer months, and they are a must year-round for those who chill easily. You can rent a wet suit your first couple of times on the water (when you rent a board), but I suggest making a wet suit one of your first surfing investments.

Wet-suit technology has come a long way. Wet suits are now thinner, have more elasticity, and keep you warmer than they did in the past. There are a few wet-suit styles, but the most common are full and spring suits. A full suit has long sleeves and full-length legs for cool- to cold-water surfing. It should cover all the way to your wrists and ankles. A spring suit has short sleeves and short legs, and it's for the summer months or more tropical waters. It keeps you slightly warmer than just a swimsuit alone. When you try on a wet suit it should feel tight but allow you a full range of motion. There should be some give to the material, but it shouldn't bag in any spots.

Wet suits come in a variety of thicknesses, which are measured in millimeters. Full suits can have different thicknesses for the center and extremities of your body. For example, a 3/2 is three millimeters thick in the chest and back and two millimeters in the legs and arms. A 3/2 is a good suit for water temperatures in the 60s, like Southern California's spring and fall. A 4/3 would be more appropriate in colder climates when water temps dip into the 50s, like winter in northern Florida through the Carolinas. Spring suits only have one thickness (usually 2 millimeters).

Recent models are more elastic in the shoulders, so they are easier to paddle in than their more antiquated versions. The thicker the suit, the more fabric you are fighting when you paddle, so if you need a thicker suit, go ahead and invest in one that advertises good flexibility in the arms. Girls usually chill more easily than the guys, so don't feel bad if your suit is thicker than your guy friends'; it's all about practicality.

An added benefit of wearing a wet suit year-round is that it protects your skin from the sun. You'll get a lot of color sitting on the water for hours at a time, and you'll want to protect your skin as much as possible so that you keep it healthy!

HINT Wet suits for surfing *always* zip up in the back. Period.

CARE

Wet suits will cost you anywhere from $100 to $400. As the water gets colder, you will realize what an important investment a wet suit can be. Take good care of your wet suit and make it last longer by rinsing it out with cool, clean water after every use and hanging it out to dry. Do not hang your wet suit in direct sunlight. Turn it inside out and instead of putting it on a hanger, drape it over a railing or on a laundry rack. Be sure to dry your suit completely after each use to discourage bacteria growth. When your wet suit gets that not-so-fresh feeling, you can wash it in a bucket with a wet-suit rinse, which you can purchase at most surf shops, or try a homemade white-vinegar rinse (mix vinegar with three parts water). It's smelly but will kill off bacteria.

HINT Most wet-suit manufacturers will guarantee their stitching for the life of your suit. Check that out when you purchase one, since seams do tend to come out after a lot of use and some companies will repair them for free!

BOOTIES

As the water starts getting colder, you may want to consider investing in a pair of booties. They're kind of like thick rubber socks for surfing, and they'll keep your toes warm all winter long. There are two kinds: split-toe and solid (round-toe). The split-toe bootie gives you more control on the board but has the disadvantage of occasionally snagging your leash in between your big and second toe. The full bootie has a simple round toe. Split-toe and round-toe booties are mostly a matter of your personal comfort. A perk of booties is that pedicures are often ruined by walking on the sand or rocks, and booties will protect that perfect polish job!

Care for your booties the same way you do your wet suit. Because they are thick and don't allow for good air flow, they take a while to dry and can get stinky fast. Try the white-vinegar trick mentioned earlier. It works!

HOODS AND GLOVES

Hoods and gloves are also useful in cold-water situations. Hoods fit snugly and keep your head and ears warm when the temps drop below the mid-50s. They are usually made of an elastic material like neoprene (similar to your wet suit). Hoods cover your head, neck, and chin and either tuck into, lie on top of, or snap into your wet suit. Wet suits that are 4/3 millimeters or thicker are usually available with a built-in or removable hood. More compact hoods, called caps, cover your head and ears and attach under your chin. Gloves, also usually made of neoprene and rubber, keep your hands and fingers warm in cold-water conditions. Some thinner gloves are also webbed to help facilitate your paddling.

WARNING There is certainly a risk of head injury, mostly from other boards flying at you out in the water, but there is also the risk that you could hit the reef or rocks. Water-use helmets (there are a couple made for surfing, wakeboarding, and kayaking), which look similar to bike and skateboard helmets, can be worn. However, these aren't very popular, and learning proper safety techniques (check out the Etiquette and Safety chapter) might be another answer. But if Mom says you have to, then you have to.

Surf Bag Essentials

Having your bag packed and ready makes it easy to head out the door and go surfing anytime the mood strikes you. Your bag should include (but is not limited to):

A towel
Sunscreen (for body and face)
Sun-protective lip balm
A hairbrush or comb
Extra hair bands if you have long hair
A change of clothes
Surf wax/wax comb
Surf leash (if you don't keep it fastened to your board)
Fin key (tightens your surfboard's fins as they become loose from use; I have yet to need mine but have had the opportunity to lend it to cute boys in the parking lot)
Tide book (a year's list of local tides)
Bottled water (one to drink and a larger one for rinsing off in case there are no showers)
Energy bar or other healthy snack

Getting Wet

There are a few basic ways to learn how to surf. One, which I strongly recommend, is by attending a surf school or surf camp in your area. I find this to be the safest way to learn in the most controlled environment. Just one or two days is enough to get a feel for surfing, learn the basics, and practice safety measures so you can head out with your buddies with some experience under your belt. You can also take a private lesson if you can't stand the idea of your fellow grommets seeing you flail around in the water. Another option is to go out with friends who are willing to teach you, but I have heard more than a handful of stories of people being injured or just plain frustrated and giving up surfing after only one try.

SURF SCHOOLS

I seriously recommend taking at least a day or weekend class to begin your surfing career. Surf school instructors teach you the basics. They will take you out in the water and put you on big foam surfboards (as opposed to a hard fiberglass board), so it's nearly impossible to hurt yourself! The nice thing is that there are now many all-girl surf schools that are low pressure, with no competition, and you can make a complete ass out of yourself without any potential boyfriends watching. They also supply you with a board and wet suit, so you can get a taste of surfing without committing to buying any equipment. You can look in the Resources section of this book, go online, or ask at your local surf shop for schools in your area. Call the school or e-mail them with any questions. If they make you feel comfortable over the phone, they will most likely make you comfortable in the water.

WHAT TO EXPECT

You'll need to book ahead because the most popular surf schools fill up fast. Prices vary, but be prepared to pay anywhere from $50 to $100 a day. Women and girls of all ages are in attendance, so no matter what your age, get out there! Some people attend with friends, but many women are there alone, so if you can't persuade a buddy to join you, don't hesitate.

You will probably need to show up early in the morning, since that is the time when there is the least amount of wind, which makes the water choppy. Sunrise is the ideal time to surf—ouch!—but most schools will start around 8:00 A.M. There is usually a one-hour session on the beach, where your instructors will go over safety, etiquette, and the fundamentals of surfing. You will probably practice your "pop-ups" (maneuvering from a lying to a standing position on your board) on the beach a couple of times, and then it will be time to hit the water!

The first day, the instructors will probably take you out in groups to catch a little white water, where it's easier to stand up on your board. Catching white water is the first step in learning how to surf. Here, the wave will break behind you (you'll be facing the shore), catch you and your board, and bring you straight into shore. If you are at a good, long break you should have enough time to stand up. Once you get up and ride one into shore, I promise you will be hooked!

The second day you might go out a little farther into the ocean. The real goal of surfing is to get on the wave before it breaks and ride it along the face, always inches ahead of the white water. This is *much* harder. It will take many tries and lots of balance, strength, and wave knowledge. Don't be frustrated if you can't do this the first or even the second day. It takes most of us months to perfect this skill.

PRIVATE LESSONS

You may not be able to find a surf school or camp in your area, so check the Internet or local surf shop for a list of private instructors. Taking a private lesson is great. You get all the attention, you go at your own speed, and there is always someone with an eye on you. Do a little research on the instructor; and if you are paying good money, make sure he or she has the proper equipment for you to use. He should be able to supply you with a wet suit and board (make sure it is a foam longboard), and he should also be trained in CPR and/or as a lifeguard. And, of course, expect to pay a little more—usually around $100 for a two-hour lesson.

With a private or class lesson under your belt, you will be well on your way to becoming a surfer. You can choose either to continue taking lessons or start braving it on your own, with a buddy of course! It's all practice, practice, practice.

GOING OUT WITH FRIENDS

So your friends have promised to take you out and show you the ropes. If they offer up a board for you to use, make sure it's a longboard. Longboards are infinitely easier to begin on than shortboards. Let me say it again, if you are just getting started, use a longboard, the longer the board, the better (8 to 10 feet is best). They are easier to paddle, easier to stand up on, and more stable. Your shortboarding friends may pooh-pooh you, but I promise you, you will have a better time of it. If your friends don't have a longboard to offer, you can rent one at many surf shops (anywhere from $10 to $30 an hour). For your first couple of tries I recommend getting a foam surfboard. Yes, you will call attention to your novice status, but we have all gone through it, and you won't get any unsightly bruises when your board hits you, which it undoubtedly will.

If it's your very first time surfing, make sure your friends are really going to give you a lesson and not just leave you alone to figure it out on your own. They don't need to be the best surfers in the world, although it would certainly help, but they should have all their attention focused on you during the lesson. Surfers are notoriously selfish and if the waves look good, they may leave you to go catch some rides, so make sure you're with someone you trust. Once you've absorbed the basics after a couple of surf sessions with an experienced friend, you will be able to practice with other newbie pals.

HINT Don't head out all alone until you are an accomplished surfer and totally familiar with the break.

CHAPTER II

Gear (THE ABSOLUTE NECESSITIES)

$\mathcal{T}$ HE GREAT THING about the sport is that once you are outfitted, it is completely free (aside from those pesky parking tickets)!

Boards

While boards come in all different sizes and styles, they almost always have similar properties. Most surfboards are shaped out of a polyurethane foam blank and then covered with fiberglass laminated with a polyester or epoxy resin. The front of the board is called the nose, and the back of the board, the tail; the top of the board is called the deck, and the sides are called the rails. The stringer runs down the center of the board for added strength. The fins are the rudderlike devices on the bottom, toward the tail, and they help stabilize, control, and maneuver the board.

Renting or borrowing a board is great for your initial foray into surfing, but sooner than later you are going to want your own. Getting your own board will help you improve faster because you will not have to adjust to different boards each time you go out (you have enough to worry about with different wave conditions; different boards just add another wrinkle to the equation). Selecting your first board is such an important choice. There are size, maneuverability, and aesthetics to consider!

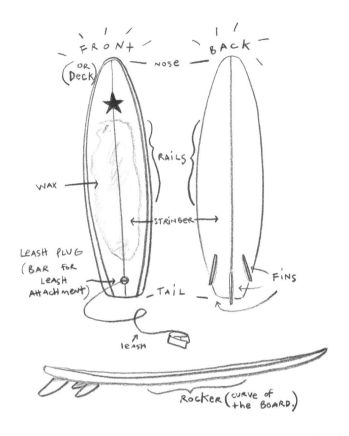

FRONT (OR DECK) — NOSE — BACK

RAILS

WAX

STRINGER

LEASH PLUG (BAR FOR LEASH ATTACHMENT)

TAIL

FINS

leash

ROCKER (CURVE of the BOARD.)

First you will need to decide if you want a longboard or a shortboard. Again, I cannot stress enough how much easier longboards are to begin with than shortboards. Even if you see a future in shortboarding, at least spend your first couple of months on a longboard. And by long, I mean 8 to 10 feet. It will seem enormous when you hold it up next to you at the surf shop, but when you take it out in the water, you will be much happier. The guy at the surf shop may say a foot taller than you is plenty; but I beg you—call me, e-mail me—from personal experience, I believe anything less than 8 or 9 feet will put you at a disadvantage. (However, if you are ten years old and weigh 60 pounds, yes, you can sacrifice length by trading it for thickness and/or width.)

LONGBOARDS VS. SHORTBOARDS

Longboards are designed for speed and accessibility to a wide range of waves, whereas shortboards are all about performance. You will see more women, children, and older surfers on longboards. They are much easier to paddle because you will get more glide per stroke than on a shortboard, and they are more stable, making balancing much easier. They are also better for riding slow-moving waves and smaller breaks. The chances of catching these kinds of waves on a shortboard could lead to frustration and temper tantrums. And it's always nice to have a longboard in your quiver for days when you will need more length and speed to catch smaller, mushier waves.

However, if you envision yourself cracking off the lips and pulling aerials, a shortboard is for you. It's harder to paddle and ride but infinitely more maneuverable. It is good for fast breaks.

There are a myriad of other boards between these two, such as hybrids (longer than a shortboard but shorter than a longboard), fish (short, fat boards for speed and maneuverability on small waves), big guns (long, narrow boards with a pointy nose for big-wave riding), and swallowtails (split-tail surfboards, which allow for looser turning). As you master surfing, you will learn more of what each of these has to offer. But for now let's just concentrate on longboards and shortboards.

See your first surfboard the way you did your first car. Although you may want to take out a Porsche immediately, it is probably best to start on an old Honda. High-performance boards and shortboards are like the Porsche in that they are going to be harder to tame, and although they may seem more attractive, they are more difficult to use. Also, in the beginning you are going to do some damage to your board—you'll get dings or cracks in it—there's no avoiding it. It would be a shame to damage a beautiful and expensive brand-new board. So buy the old, beat-up longboard and ride it until you have mastered it. Once you outgrow it, you will always be able to sell it to another beginner. Don't think of this as your only surfboard, think of it as your first!

COST

Surfboards can be *très cher*. Most run anywhere from $350 to $600. I suggest getting a used one as your first board until you know exactly what your needs will be. Used boards have a pretty high resale rate and should cost from $150 to $450, depending on their condition. In most surf shops you will find a section of used boards.

WHAT TO LOOK FOR IN A USED BOARD

Make sure there are no major dings or cracks in the board, or too much previous heavy repair work (it could weigh the board unevenly). You can tell just by looking at it—discolored patches reveal past repair work. Run your hands along the rails to make sure they are smooth and even. Pressure dings are okay (you'll notice their indentation and discoloration on the board), but cracks running all the way down to the foam should be avoided because they will absorb water. However, if the board is the right price, you could get these fixed at a surf repair shop.

HINT Because longboards are so long and wide (usually about 22 inches), it's hard for us girls to carry the board under one arm (board tucked under your armpit; hand holding the bottom rail). Try it out in the store before you purchase the board. Carrying your board with one arm is not something that is necessary, but if you have found the right board *and* can carry it this way, it is a nice perk. Trust me—not all surf spots are next to where you park your car, and the more intrepid you become, the farther you will have to walk.

CARE

Care for all of your equipment by rinsing it off with cool, clean water when you get home. Try to store your board indoors, ideally in your garage or shed. (If you leave your board out in the sun, it will yellow and could fracture more easily.) Leave your board facedown so that if the wax melts, it will drip right off and not pool on the board, making your wax messy and uneven. You can either stack your boards on the floor, or if you have the space, get wall racks. If you have to leave your board outside, place a tarp over it, even in the shade, so it doesn't get dirty or too much sun.

DINGS

Dings (cracks or breaks in your board) are inevitable. They're just a part of surfing. Your board will crash into other boards, the reef, rocks; or you'll drop it. You won't even know how some show up; they just magically appear. A ding fairy? Perhaps. Do your best to prevent dings by keeping your board in your car (if it fits), getting a board bag or sock, and holding on to your board out in the water. Sorry, but there's no way of avoiding dings altogether.

There are a couple of ways to repair your board. If you take your board to the folks at your local surf shop, they will usually send it out for repairs. If you can find out where they send it, you may get a better price or quicker service by bringing it to them directly. Or you can learn how to repair dings yourself. It will probably get to this point if you surf a lot, since you will find yourself hauling your board back and forth to the repair shop more times than you care to mention. There are all kinds of dings—one occurs when the fiberglass shatters but doesn't reach the core of the board; another is a puncture that goes all the way to the foam. In the case of damage, such as gaping holes, fins that have snapped off, or other intimidating situations, you should bring your board to the repair shop (unless you have decided a career in surfboard shaping is for you). But when it comes to shatters or little punctures, you can attempt to fix them yourself.

HINT Epoxy boards (boards finished with epoxy resin as opposed to the more standard polyester resin) are far more ding-resistant, but the boards themselves are more expensive and, at the moment, they are more expensive to repair.

QUICK DING-REPAIR LESSON

You will need solar resin (premixed resin that dries in the sun and is available at most surf shops), masking tape, a filter mask (those funny white ones that you can buy at the hardware store), sand paper (100 grit), rubber gloves and goggles, and a plastic sheet or flat wooden stick.

Make sure the area is completely dry (you may need to let your board dry out for a couple of days). Put on the filter mask, rubber gloves, and goggles. (Tiny little glass particles will be floating around during sanding, and you should avoid getting them in your lungs or eyes.) Clear the area of any loose debris and then sand the ding and about a quarter inch around it. Mark off the section with masking tape so that it doesn't get messy all around the wound. Squeeze in the resin and smooth it out with a stick, or cover it with a plastic sheet and smooth it underneath. Then let the sun work its magic. Remove the plastic sheet after it starts to set (usually one or two minutes). In five or ten minutes, when it is completely dry (not tacky anymore), sand the area until it's totally smooth. If you are a perfectionist, you may want to go up in grades of sandpaper to get the perfect finish.

Bags and Socks

Once you get a fancy new board, you may want to protect it with a board bag or a board sock. Both will protect it from dings out of the water. Socks, which are usually made out of a stretchy cotton fabric with a nylon nose piece and a drawstring closure, are better than nothing, but they might not be as easy or convenient as a board bag with a zipper. Board bags are made of a polypropylene material, have a zipper closure to get your bag in and out, and often come with a sturdy strap. Mark one side of your bag or sock to indicate the waxed side—this way you won't get the bottom of your board covered in wax. Plus, if you are planning to take your board with you while you travel, you'll need to get a board bag. Remove the fins and pack a towel around your board or put your clothes in with it to protect it from breaking.

Car Racks

There are two kinds of car racks: hard and soft. The hard racks are semi-permanent and stay on your car year-round. Soft racks are put on and taken off as you use them. Consider how often you will be surfing to see which is a better choice for you. If you surf twice or more a week, it is probably better to get hard racks. On newer cars your manufacturer probably makes a good rack that fits neatly onto your car. Otherwise, Thule's and Yakima's are best (but pricey!). If you have a car that already has factory-installed crossbars on it but no attachments for your surfboard, you will need to purchase a pad-and-strap combo such as a Rac Roll. This is a padded roll that attaches to your crossbar with straps that go around the bar and over your surfboard. They attach with either a plastic or metal clasp. There are a bunch of different kinds; ask at your local surf shop about the best one for your car. You may want to have one of the surf shop employees show you how to put it on the first time. Surf rack directions can be vague.

If you have an older car with a rain gutter, there are great hard racks that screw on to your rain gutter. They hold well and are easy to use. There are a couple of brands, but the classic Snubber can be found online or at most surf shops.

There are two types of soft racks: those that hook on to your rain gutters or those that go all the way around your roof. Both can be stowed in the trunk or garage and take up little space. Soft racks are not as secure as hard racks.

USING YOUR RACKS

Center your board on your racks, deck (or top) down. There is great debate about placing fins forward or back. I personally like to put them forward so that if the straps loosen and the board slips back, there's the slim chance that the fins will catch on the strap and give me a couple more precious seconds to pull over. When stacking boards, place a towel between them in order to cushion and protect them from getting wax on one another.

WARNING Be safe about stacking boards. Know your racks and don't pile on too many. Soft racks, or even some rack rolls with plastic attachments, aren't great for freeway driving. If you use a soft rack, get extra straps and suggestions from surf shops in your area. Be safe. Losing your board to the asphalt is one thing; hurting the person driving behind you is another.

And you should know that your surfboard isn't protected from theft on your car rack. Always keep your eye on your parked car.

Leashes

In 1970, Jack O'Neill fastened a length of surgical tubing to the nose of his board and looped the other end around his wrist. The surf leash was born. (Jack lost his eye a year later when his board snapped back and hit him in the face—presumably, this first leash material was too elastic.)

There are a couple kinds of leashes, and as a beginner, you should absolutely use one. You will notice some longboarders out there who don't wear leashes in order to do tricks like walking the board or hanging ten, but you're not there yet. You need yours so that you don't spend hours chasing your board into shore, where it could knock out unsuspecting beachgoers.

Your leash should be approximately the same length as your board (9-foot board, 9-foot leash). The leash will usually come with a separate tie that you loop around the leash plug (the little bar near the tail of your board that is built into all new boards). You then attach the small Velcro side of your leash to the tie. You can leave your leash attached or take it off when not in use. The other end of the leash, with the ankle strap, goes around the ankle of your *back* foot (the foot closer to the tail). There are also leashes that go around your knee for longboarders who don't want to trip as they walk the board. Put the Velcro strap around your ankle or knee securely with the leash attachment on the outside of your leg before you paddle out.

HINT When surfing over a reef or craggy rocks, keep your leash pulled up, hold it over your shoulder, or tuck the excess under your leg. Otherwise, it could get caught on the reef and pull you down. In case you do get snagged, pull the strap off your ankle immediately and maneuver from there. If you are surfing over sand, it's okay to just let your leash float in the water.

Why Wax?

Shaving your legs is up to you, but waxing your board is essential. It keeps your feet from slipping while you are surfing.

Basecoat is a wax that you put down on a freshly cleaned or brand-new board. This helps your topcoat stick better. Put a thin, even coat all over the deck of your board from the tail to about a foot or two below the nose.

Next is the topcoat (which is also referred to simply as surf wax). There are a few types of topcoats and the one you use depends on the water temperature in your area. Cold is for water temps below 60 degrees (brrr!), cool is for 58 to 68 degrees, warm is for 64 to 74, and tropical is for water temperatures over 75 degrees.

Put a generous amount of topcoat over the basecoat. (If you don't have basecoat, don't worry about it too much; it's not absolutely necessary—just double up on the topcoat.) The goal is to have the wax form little bumps on your board. You are going to have to push down pretty firmly on your board to get the bumps, so do it on grass, or try to hold your board on your lap while you do it. Never do it on asphalt because you could crack your glassing (skin of your board). And doing it on the beach might get sand in your wax, which could scratch your skin. The wax will wear off after a couple of surf sessions, so reapply by adding more wax on top of the existing wax.

You can purchase surf wax at almost any surf shop. Wax bars (top and base) will cost you about a dollar a bar. The available brands are pretty comparable. Just pick the scent that most appeals to you!

You will need to remove the wax and then rewax your clean board only when the wax loses its stickiness or gets sandy or excessively dirty (every couple of weeks or months, depending on use). In order to remove the existing wax, place the board in the sun for about ten minutes (aiming a hair dryer at your board will work just as well on overcast days). Make sure you leave your board in the direct sunlight for the shortest amount of time it takes to soften the wax (to prevent sun damage). This trick will save you hours. Don't try to take the wax off without heating it; it will just make you crazy. Once heated, wax will become soft and you can simply wipe it off with the bevel side of a wax comb. (If you don't have a wax comb, a paint scraper will do.) Scrape off the wax first and then use a wax remover (acetone) to remove the dregs of wax that can't be scraped off with a wax comb. Wax remover can be picked up in most surf shops.

A wax comb has a bevel on one side (which is used as previously described) and a comb on the other. The comb is not for your hair! Use the comb when the surface of the wax on your board has lost its stickiness. Scrape the wax with the comb to agitate it and expose the stickier wax underneath. Pick up a wax comb when you make your first purchase of surf wax.

If there is just a little wax residue on the bottom of your surfboard after having boards stacked together on top of your car, take a handful of sand and rub the bottom of your board to remove it. (Bumps of wax on the bottom of your board could slow you down as you glide through the water.)

HINT A Wet Box or a Wet/Dry Bag is great if you are not lucky enough to be able to walk to the beach and you have to cart your gear around in your (or your mom's) nice clean car. For a Wet Box, choose any plastic box with a snap-on lid and no holes in the bottom or sides. Rubbermaid makes a bunch of them. Get one with a 19-quart capacity or bigger. A Wet/Dry bag is great in that it lets water out and air in, so you don't get mildew and its stinky smell! Both are great for carrying damp wet suits, bathing suits, and leashes.

CHAPTER III

Surfing 101 —A VERY BRIEF HOW-TO

I CONTEND THAT YOU CAN'T POSSIBLY LEARN to surf by reading a how-to section of a book, but here are a couple of pointers that will help the beginner who can't wait to get out in the water.

I have one secret to share with you. Surfing isn't just about standing up on your board. What is more important are timing and wave knowledge. It isn't that hard to stand up (it's not easy, but it's not the greatest challenge). Anyone with a little bit of balance and natural athleticism shouldn't have much trouble standing on a long foam board that is riding through the white water. The secret of surfing, and what it's truly about, is being in that sweet spot on the wave, taking off and always being right where the wave is breaking, adjusting your speed so that you are just ahead of the white water coming down the face of the wave, never too far ahead and never too far back. It is in this spot where you can perform tricks and maneuvers or simply just hang out. This is the part that takes great wave knowledge and lots of practice. Whether you are in this spot on a surfboard or boogie board, standing up or lying down, you are surfing.

HINT Anyone who has ever seen Jesse Billauer surf could tell you that surfing isn't about standing. Jesse became a quadriplegic in a surfing accident, but with the help of his pro-surfer friends Jesse still gets out there and surfs by lying on a specialized surfboard and riding the wave.

Get Up Early

Sorry, late sleepers, but you are going to have to get up early to catch the best waves and avoid the late-day choppy water that makes it harder to paddle and creates a bumpy ride when you do actually catch a wave.

Finding the Right Waves and the Right Breaks

Breaking waves all have similar characteristics. There is the face, or the green part of the wave, which is the unbroken, sloping section of a wave (this is where more advanced surfers ride). Once a wave breaks, it produces white water (this is where the beginner will ride to get a feel for surfing and practice standing up). The top of the wave is known as the

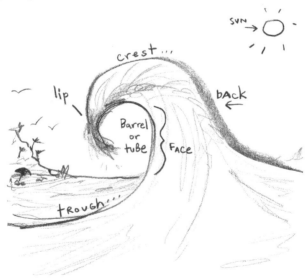

crest; the bottom is the trough. If a wave pitches forward and out when it breaks, it produces a barrel or tube (not all waves do this).

Getting started on the right kind of wave is key! Ideally, you would find a wave that peels, meaning it starts breaking in one spot and then continues breaking outward as it approaches shore. A point break (where waves break predictably in one spot and then peel out in the same direction) will almost always supply you with this kind of wave, but point breaks are often crowded with experienced surfers. At a point break everyone has to take off from pretty much the same spot, which can leave you sitting there twiddling your thumbs while the more advanced surfers slip right by you and pick up every wave.

A beach break is a better place to get started, but you must go during the right conditions. What you *don't* want is a day when the waves are closed out. "Closed out" means the entire wave breaks at once from end to end. When you take off on a closed-out wave of decent size, you will most likely end up "over the falls" (getting picked up and thrown over in the curl) and going through "the washing machine" (getting tumbled around under water). It's not as much fun as it sounds. A good day at a beach break will supply you with peeling waves that have shoulders (the green face ahead of where the wave is breaking).

Scope out locations for a beginner break. If an area looks scary from the shore, it probably is. As a beginner you'll be spending a lot of time paddling (belly on the board, hands in the water), and your head will be only a couple of inches off the board. So even the smallest wave can be intimidating. Look around. If there are other beginners or kids at a particular spot, you should be okay. If there is a guy pulling aerials with a shortboard that says, "Groms, go home!" you should choose another location.

HINT Surfing is a little scary but shouldn't put you into a full panic. It's okay to be nervous, but if you truly feel uncomfortable out there, feel free to call it a day.

On the Beach

SIT AND WATCH THE WAVES

See where they break. Check where more advanced surfers take off and imagine yourself doing the same. Find a spot that's less crowded and decide if you are going to sit on the inside and just surf on the white water or attempt to go out farther into the lineup. You can see the whole picture from shore; it is harder to gauge it when you are out in the water.

STRETCH OUT

Start with a couple of stretches to warm up your paddling muscles. Concentrate on your arms, shoulders, back, and legs. Hold all stretches for fifteen to thirty seconds.

I usually start with forward bends. Legs apart, reach your arms behind you and clasp your hands together behind your back. Roll your shoulders down and back. Bend at your waist and move into a forward bend. Now upside down, reach your arms, hands still clasped, toward the ground until you feel a good stretch in your shoulders and hamstrings.

Release your hands and reach over to one side, holding on to your leg, stretching your back and sides. Then stretch over to the other leg. Come up slowly.

With your legs still apart, while keeping your left hand on your hip, lean over to the left side with your right arm reaching overhead; now do the other side. This will give you a good stretch through your sides.

To stretch your shoulders, cross your right arm over to the left side of your body and keep it parallel with the ground. Using your left hand, pull your arm in tight until you feel a stretch in your right shoulder. Now try the other side.

Stretch your triceps by starting with your right arm straight up overhead. Bending at your elbow, bring down your hand and place your palm flat against your back. With your left hand, pull your elbow gently toward your head until you feel the stretch. Change sides.

Perform any other stretches like calf or neck stretches or simple twists that will make you feel water-ready!

PRACTICE YOUR POP-UPS

You will use the pop-up out in the water after you've caught a wave to get from lying down to standing on your board. Before you get in the water, practice your pop-up on the beach. Lay down your board in the soft sand (make sure to do this on soft sand and not in your living room or you will hurt your board and fin). Lie facedown on your board, feet at the tail. Pretend you are paddling and then, in one motion, with hands near your rails straighten your arms, and at the same time pull both feet forward, so they're under your shoulders. Land with one foot forward and one in back over the center line of your board. Keep them slightly wider than shoulder width apart. Your back foot will be approximately a foot up from the tail and perpendicular to the length of your board. Your front foot should be out at a slight angle. Your body will be facing sideways, but you'll look forward. Keep your knees slightly bent, since these will be your shock absorbers.

HINT Whew, that's a lot to think about when you are out in the water! Try pop-ups at home on the floor without your board so that you get used to the motion.

In the Water

WALK OUT

Walk your board out as far as you can into the water, keeping it by your side (never in front of you). Shuffle your feet if there is a sandy bottom to make sure you don't step on any ocean life. When you see that not many waves are coming in, jump on your board and paddle out. If you are somewhere with a rocky or reefy bottom, you may not be able to walk out and you may need to start paddling earlier. Just make sure to be in water deep enough that your fin doesn't drag along the bottom.

HINT If you are walking out over a shallow rocky area, flip your board over so the fin is facing up. The buoyancy of the board will keep it afloat and give you something to lean on, and you will protect your fin. Flip it back over once you're far enough out in the water.

PADDLING

When you're on your board, use only your arms to paddle. Don't kick with your feet. Using a freestyle stroke, alternate your arms and cup your hands to push as much water out from under you, giving you as much speed as possible. It's best to use long, deep strokes and bring your hands slightly under the sides of your board. Keep your head and chest arched up and your legs together on the board. You also want to keep your board trim with the water. This means your board lies flat without the nose or tail popping up. (If your fins are dragging or your nose is underwater, it will slow you down.) To do this, find the sweet spot on your board that keeps you level (your body will usually be slightly off center toward the tail). There are usually logos or stickers right about where your head should be. As you paddle, find the place where you are most level and then see where you are on your board. Maybe your nose is over the sticker or your chest is in line with the emblem. The next time you get on your board, try to line yourself back up in that spot.

At a reef or point break, paddle out around the break. At beach breaks you will need to paddle out through some white water. You may be able to catch a ride out on a rip current (look for water that looks dirty—that's your key). If you are paddling and paddling and can't get out, sometimes it helps to come back in and try another location. Follow another surfer out—but not too closely because a wave could drag the surfer and her board back into you.

GETTING THROUGH THE WAVES

At most spots you will encounter broken waves and the white water coming at you while you paddle out. As you may know from playing in the ocean, the white water can pick you up and drag you right back to shore, so the best thing to do to hold your ground is to go *under* the wave.

There are a couple of ways to get through the white water. The easiest way is to do a push-up on your board. If it is just a small amount of white water rushing at you, push up into the top of a push-up position, hands on the rails. This will make your board go under the white water and your body will go over it. The goal is to not lose any ground.

If this doesn't work, the more popular ways of getting out include "turtling" and "duck diving." If you are on a longboard (and you should be as a beginner!), you will need to turtle roll. To do this, think of a turtle and as the white water approaches you, hold tightly to the rails of your board, roll over onto your side and then onto your back, holding your board tightly above you. Now you are upside down underwater with the board on top of you. The white water will pass over you and your board. After you feel the wave pass, flip over, get back on your board, and continue paddling. You may have to do this a couple of times to get out past the breaking waves.

If you are on a shorter, lighter board, you can duck dive. In this instance, you will grab your rails and push the nose of your board under the wave. Put your knee on the center of your board to get it all the way under water. This should get you under and out to the other side of the wave. It takes a lot of strength to do this move, and you may not be able to do it unless you are on a super lightweight board. If you don't have enough body weight or strength to push your board under the wave, stick with the turtle roll.

WARNING Once you pass the white water and you're right where the waves are breaking, you'll be at the impact zone. This is a bad place to be. If you paddle forward, the wave will most likely take you up with it and flip you back into the water. Or if you stay put (like the deer in the headlights), you will take one on the head. There is no good solution here. You can hold on to your board and pray, or if *no one* is around, you may ditch your board and dive under the wave (just don't get in the habit). Also, try to gauge your speed better the next time in order to get through this area during a lull. The idea is to get past this spot as quickly as possible.

SITTING

Once you are out past the break, sit up on your board. This will give you the greatest advantage for seeing incoming waves. Center yourself on the middle of your board with it lying flat on the water and your legs dangling over either side. You will sit facing out toward the horizon watching for the forming waves (they look like dark shadows in the water). When you see one coming toward you, scoot your butt way back on your board so the nose of the board comes all the way out of the water. Hold the rail on the side in the direction you are turning and eggbeater your legs while using your free hand to stroke the water and turn you toward shore. Once you are facing land, lie down on your board. Keep checking back over your shoulder to make sure the wave is coming and paddle toward shore like crazy.

Riding

WHITE WATER

If you are just starting out, don't be ashamed to just ride the white water. Here you will sit on the "inside," which means in between where the waves are breaking and the shore, but far enough from shore that you can get in a decent ride. Then turn your board toward shore and wait until the wave breaks behind you. As the white water rushes toward you, paddle until the white water picks up you and your board. As soon as you feel your board pitching forward without any help from you, try your pop-up. If crawling up is easier, that is fine, too (but only in the beginning). Do whatever you can to end up standing. Riding the white water is a great way to practice surfing.

GREEN WAVE

An unbroken wave is also called a green wave. As mentioned earlier, the goal of surfing is to catch the wave before it breaks and ride along the face (or the green part of the wave) just in front of the white water. To

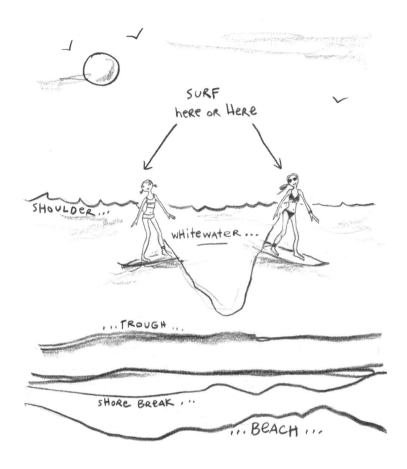

SURF here or Here

SHOULDER...

WHITEWATER...

...TROUGH...

SHORE BREAK...

...BEACH...

catch a wave in this spot, when you see a swell line coming toward you, point your board toward shore and start paddling like mad. Sometimes you will get left behind; sometimes you will "pearl" (meaning you flip forward, toes going over your nose). Adjust yourself farther back or forward on the board accordingly; arching your back up will also help you be perfectly balanced. Once you feel the wave pick you up, give one more strong paddle and then try your pop-up. Now you're surfing!

Just keep playing around in the water to learn how each wave shapes up, where it breaks, and what its speed is. Different breaks have very different wave qualities, and you will have to spend lots of time out there getting to know each one.

WIPEOUT

Wiping out is just part of surfing. You will wipe out on every ride until you learn to "kick out" (exit the wave by riding up and over the top) or lie back down onto your board. Remember that the water is soft. Don't be afraid—relax. As a beginner, the breaks you are at won't hold you underwater for long, so don't panic. If you know you're going to fall, try to fall off to the side or back of your board; don't fall off in front of it.

GINGERBREAD MAN

When you fall off your board, fall off gingerbread-man style. Try to land flat on the water by belly flopping or back flopping. This way you won't sink too deep (you never know the depth of the water you are in or if there are rocks under you). Don't jump off feet first, because you may sprain your ankle in shallow water or jump down on something sharp. And certainly don't dive off—ouch! I don't even want to think about it.

EMERGENCY DRILL

After a fall, *always* come up with your arms over your head the way you did in those old school-emergency drills. Keep your hands behind your head and the bulk of your upper arms protecting your face. This way, if someone's board, or yours, is above you, you will walk away with a bruised arm instead of a concussion. This is *muy importante!*

COMING IN

No need to paddle yourself in. Just wait for some white water and ride your board on your belly into shore. But be careful if there is a wicked shore break that could throw you down or rip the board out of your hands, and time your exit so that you get out during a lull.

Surfers ARE NOT THE ONLY ONES CATCHING A RIDE. HERE ARE SOME OF THE OTHER PEOPLE WE SHARE OUR WAVES WITH:

BODYSURFERS

Bodysurfers ride the ocean waves with only the use of their own bodies (and sometimes swim fins). By swimming into either breaking waves or white water, bodysurfers try to harness the power of the waves and ride them into shore.

BODYBOARDERS (AKA BOOGIE BOARDERS)

Bodyboarders ride a buoyant foam board approximately $3\frac{1}{2}$ feet in length. They usually ride lying down or drop-knee style (a kneeling stance with one knee down) and often wear swim fins to help them paddle out and get them into a wave. Where surfers paddle with their arms, bodyboarders kick with their legs.

CANOE AND KAYAK SURFERS

Riding either an outrigger canoe or a kayak, these surfers truly paddle in by muscling their boats into a wave with either single or double-bladed paddles.

PADDLEBOARDING

Also out in the ocean, but not in the actual breaking waves, are paddleboarders. Paddleboarding is like surfing in that you get around by paddling with your arms on specifically designed boards, which are similar to surfboards, but they're thicker and more buoyant. Except the boards aren't designed for wave riding, so the athlete doesn't do the actual stand-up surfing part. Why would you do this, you may ask yourself? Paddleboarders are often surfers, and the sport is great for endurance and strength training.

And don't forget, dolphins, seals, and pelicans ride waves with more skill and grace than we ever will.

CHAPTER IV

Etiquette and Safety

Etiquette

SINCE WE'RE GIRLS, WE GET AWAY with a heck of a lot more out there than the boys do simply by being so darn cute! But it pays to be neighborly and to know the rules of surfing. Your fellow surfers will be stoked to see you out there learning. (Don't be surprised if you get a round of applause when you catch your first wave.) More advanced surfers will be able to avoid you, but you should know the rules so you can at least say "my bad" when getting in the way of other surfers. Check out the following rules and etiquette so we surfer girls can keep our squeaky clean image both in and out of the water.

DON'T DROP IN

The person farthest out from shore and closest to where the wave is breaking has the right of way. If you are farther from the breaking part of the wave, on the shoulder, and the person on the inside is catching the wave, pull back. Don't drop in. As a beginner, you can assume that anyone up on a wave has priority over you.

QUEUE UP

At point or reef breaks where there is a centralized takeoff area, there is an unofficial line. It's kind of like Disneyland—wait for those who were there before you to go, then it is your turn. Once you have taken a wave, or even attempted a ride, give those closer to the peak a chance. Let a couple of waves go by before you try again. Hopefully, others will do the same for you.

PADDLE STRAIGHT OUT

Try to paddle straight out at a beach break, avoiding the peak of the wave and the takeoff zones where surfers are beginning their ride. This is easier said than done, since the takeoff spot at a beach break can shift around because of changing sandbars and tides. This also means you may have to paddle out through the white water rather than through the unbroken sections. If surfers are coming down the line as you are paddling out, try to gauge your speed and paddle behind them. At a point or reef, try to paddle around the breaking waves.

HINT Remember, in order to get through the white water when you are paddling out, use your turtle roll or duck dive.

LOCATION, LOCATION, LOCATION

Stick to spots that support your ability level. (Beginners, don't paddle out at Pipeline.) Surfing at spots that are too difficult puts you as well as those around you in danger. That being said, more advanced surfers shouldn't get pissy with those newbies trying to learn at well-known beginner breaks. Check out some of the great beginner spots and avoid the gnarly breaks that are mentioned in Chapter XIII: Surf Spots.

DON'T DITCH YOUR BOARD

When you are turtling or duck diving, hold tightly to your board. Don't just let it go haphazardly with the wave, because you will knock out surfers behind you. Remember, you have a ring of destruction around you equal to the length of your leash! If you can't hold on—let's be honest, sometimes the wave will rip the board from your hands—try to yell "Board!" to warn other surfers that your board is riding the wave without you!

BEGINNERS ARE INVISIBLE

When more advanced surfers see beginners like you flailing around looking as if they don't have it all under control yet, they will ignore you. Fortunately, they will avoid you, but they will also ignore you—meaning they will take off when you are going for a wave, assuming that you are unable to catch it. Don't get upset—you probably weren't going to catch that wave anyway. Perhaps when they see you actually catch one, they will pull back and give a cheerful hoot!

RESPECT YOUR ELDERS

Older surfers have probably been surfing the break since before you were born. Give 'em some space and their fair share of waves; they may do the same for you. Don't be afraid to ask advice; more surfers than not will be flattered and eager to tell you what they know. And they have a lot to teach you; if they give you some advice (kind or unkind), be gracious and take it.

SHARE WAVES

Once you get good enough to catch most of the waves you try for, share—especially if you are on a longboard—because you will be farther out than the shortboarders and as a result, you'll be able to catch more waves. Let others have their turn, especially those who aren't as good as you. Even if you were snaked all the time when you started, don't return the favor. Surfing shouldn't be a hazing process.

LOCALISM SUCKS

But, unfortunately, it does exist. Know something about the surf spot where you are going out. It is best to go with someone who has surfed there before. Sadly, there are spots where locals will pester you, throw things, and break into your car. Some have gone so far as to beat up other surfers. This gross behavior should not be condoned, and it should be avoided, especially by the beginning surfer.

PICK UP AFTER YOURSELF

And finally, the best etiquette is to always leave the beach as you found it. Don't litter—whether you are on the beach or on the street. Join an ocean conservation philanthropy like Surfrider Foundation. We have only one planet; treat it with respect.

Safety

Here are several very important tips to keep yourself safe when you're out in the water. The ocean is an intimidating and humbling force; you cannot dominate it, but you can become familiar enough with it to handle yourself intelligently.

SWIM

You'll need to be a relatively strong swimmer in order to surf. If you haven't spent much time in the water, shape up by swimming laps in a local pool. Play in the ocean to get to know the wave strength and rip-current pull. Never be out farther than it would be possible for you to swim back in the worst-case scenario that your leash breaks and you lose your board.

OBSERVE YOUR CONDITIONS

If you're unfamiliar with a beach, take the time to observe its wave and current conditions before going in. And know your limits. Stay out of surf that is too dangerous for you to handle.

KEEP YOUR BOARD AT YOUR SIDE

When you are on the inside in the white water, always keep your board to your side and perpendicular to the beach and waves. Never have your board in front of you, because the force of the wave could push your board right into you and knock you down, knock you out, or worse. And if your board is parallel to the waves, it gives the white water more surface with which to rip your board from your hands and away from you. When your board is perpendicular, it can cut through the waves more easily because it puts less drag on the board.

NEVER TURN YOUR BACK

Ever heard the expression, "Never turn your back on young children or the ocean?" Well, there's a lot of truth in that. The ocean is totally unpredictable and can change in an instant. When your back is facing the horizon, you may not see the rogue wave coming at you or the surfer headed your way.

BUDDY SYSTEM

Always surf with a buddy. When you are just starting out, bring a friend along so you can keep an eye on each other. The truth is that even if you don't have a friend in tow, you will most likely never surf totally alone at any break. Most surfers are aware of others out in the water and will be observant. (I mean if you saw a board with no person attached, I hope you would investigate—unless you notice a big fin and a red tint to the water, in which case paddle like mad for shore and alert a lifeguard.)

LANDMARKS

Depending on the swell, you will most likely float north or south along the shore, so once in the water, look for landmarks on shore to mark your position. Keep an eye on where you started so you don't become disoriented. Also, make sure you don't get pulled too far out. Stay in line with other surfers.

KNOW WHEN TO GET OUT OF THE WAY

If another inexperienced surfer, or even an experienced surfer in need of an attitude adjustment, is coming directly at you and you don't think you can get out of the way, this is the only time you should do this: ditch your board and go under the water. They will skim over you and you won't get hit. Always be alert to this situation, though. If it is a skilled surfer, he or she can most likely go around you with no problem, even when it looks like the aim is right at your head. But it's better to be safe than sorry. The safest place is down below the surface of the water.

CLEANUP SETS

Every now and then a rogue wave will come in. It will be bigger than the rest of the sets, and it will break farther out. This is called a cleanup set because it puts all the surfers on the inside through the wash. When you see one coming, haul ass toward the horizon and you may just be able to clear it. If it breaks before you get to it, turtle roll and hold on for dear life. If *no one,* and I mean no one, is around, you may ditch your board and dive under the wave. If you can't beat it, join it—sometimes I just turn around, point my board toward shore, and ride the white water in.

GETTING HOOKED

If your leash gets snagged on coral or rock after a fall, or while you are sitting on your board, first remove the strap from your ankle and navigate from there. Because your board is more buoyant than you, it could stay up while you get pulled down. Waves could pull your board away, sinking you under the water—yikes!

HINT New leashes with quick-release straps are coming out for just this kind of situation. If you are at a location with a sea floor known for snagging leashes, you may want to invest in one.

DEHYDRATION

Be aware of dehydration and sun exposure while surfing. Drink lots of water, wear plenty of sunscreen, and when you begin to feel fatigued, get out of the water and sit in the shade.

Finally, drugs and alcohol have no place in sports or in the ocean. Drinkers are sinkers.

CHAPTER V

Be Cool

GIRLS CARRYING SURFBOARDS LOOK COOL no matter what. But here are a couple of tips to make it look like you know what you are doing even when you don't!

Substance: Looking Cool from the Parking Lot to the Water

SURF SPEAK

There is certainly a language used by surfers (check out the Glossary), but there are a few things to keep in mind to make you sound as cool as you are. Mainly, don't use too many surf words all in one sentence. Only people who don't surf will ask you, "Dude, did you catch some gnarly waves on your board?" Most surfers I know would just roll their eyes at this question. A simple "How was the surf?" would suffice and make you sound like you know what you're talking about. An example of the right answer is, "Perfect, three to four." ("Great conditions, the waves were three to four feet tall.")

When you are speaking about surfing, you are usually talking about what the ocean is doing, because that is what is going to affect your surfing conditions. What time are high and low tide? What is the height of the waves? Does a spot break on an incoming or outgoing tide? These are the topics on which surfers usually dwell (we'll cover more of this in Chapter XI: The Ocean and Surf Reports). The more you know about the ocean, the more you will be able to speak like a true surfer!

TOWEL TRICK

The towel trick is something every great surfer knows. Stand in a parking lot near a crowded surf spot and you will see many male surfers changing out of their wet suits or swim trunks and back into their shorts with nary a view of their cute behinds. Damn! How do they do it? It's the towel trick. To change from your bikini bottoms back into dry clothes, start by tying your towel tight and high around your waist so you don't pull it off with your suit. Then reach up under the towel and pull your bottoms off. Put your clothes on underneath and, voilà, not a private part shown! (You may want to practice this trick at home before braving a parking lot full of guys.) You can also do this with a wet suit worn without a bathing suit underneath, but it involves more wiggling and jiggling and careful T-shirt negotiation. Getting your bra on under your shirt is a whole different story, and I leave that up to you to figure out.

KEYS

What do you do with your car key when you go out to surf? It is well known that surfers often leave their keys tucked under the bumper of their cars, but this isn't a terribly good idea. Most wet suits and even leashes have places for your car key, so you can take it out with you, but these days many cars have electronic keys. Quite a conundrum. You usually get one key with your car that isn't electronic—try to make that your surfing key and slip it in your wet suit. Or, at your own risk, find a good hiding spot . . . shh! I won't tell.

CARRY YOUR OWN THINGS

Often you will park far away from where you surf; there may be cliffs or roads to good breaks that just aren't accessible by car. Since you don't

need much to go out surfing, leave most of your stuff in your car. That way you won't have a ton of things to juggle. Put on your wet suit and sunblock ahead of time so you don't need to carry it all down to the beach with you. You don't want to be the girl who is a burden to take out because you can't deal with your own junk. Longboards are heavy—I won't deny it—but you have to be able to carry your own board. You can carry your board a couple of ways: under one arm, if your arm is long enough to go around it and hold on to the bottom rail; on your head, balancing the weight with your hands on either rail; on your hip, holding it out to the side with your hands on both rails and weight on your hip; or on your shoulder, resting the center of the wax side of the board on your shoulder, with your arm wrapped around to hold on to the back. Dropping or dragging your board, or your friend's board, for that matter, is a super no-no! Just think, you will get strong muscles toting your board around.

WARNING Never leave your board behind a parked car. The chances of backing over it are just too great.

HINT Some surf spots are safer than others. Locals can spot a newbie from a mile away and might welcome you by breaking into your car and stealing your stuff. Know about the location before you go, and always leave your valuables at home.

KEEP IT CLEAN

Whenever you leave your board on the beach, always place it with the wax side down. The wax will melt in the sun if you leave your board faceup. And always rinse the sand off your board before placing it on your friend's car or yours. Only a kook carries around a sandy board.

WEAR YOUR LEASH

Your leash should be the last thing you put on before you get in the water and the first thing you take off when you get out. Put your leash on right at the water's edge so you don't trip over it and do a triple gainer into the beach break. Way too embarrassing. Also, dragging your leash along behind you when walking down the beach is poor form and can cause wear and tear. There are a couple of schools of thought about how to handle caring for your leash. There are those of us who tie it around the board (at least this way you will never forget it), and those who insist on taking it off entirely. When you wrap the leash around your board, the fins can nick the leash and make it break more easily. Should you decide to tie the leash around your board, do it right after you get out of the water. Keep the leash attached and loop it tightly around the board so it fits snug below the fins. Then connect it by placing the Velcro ankle strap around the loops.

ARE YOU GOOFY?

When you surf, you stand with one foot in front of the other and steer the board with your back foot. Regular footed means that you ride with your right foot in the back and your left foot forward. If you are goofy footed, you will stand with your left foot back and your right foot forward and will face the opposite way. Either is equally fine; there is no advantage to one over the other. You can tell if you are goofy or regular footed by the way you do a cartwheel. Which foot do you step out on? That will probably be your forward foot. Or try a pop-up: lie on your stomach, imagining you are getting up on a narrow surfboard, and push up so that your feet come up under you. Which foot do you naturally put forward? If you skateboard or snowboard you will already know which is your forward foot. In this case being goofy is cool!

SIT, STAY

Sit up on your board when you are out in the lineup. Don't lie down. Sit with your legs straddling the board and try to keep your weight in the center so your board lies flat on the water. Don't lie down or you will look lazy or inexperienced. You will wobble and bobble the first couple of times, but all of a sudden it will click. I promise that in no time you will be so stable you would be able to paint your nails out there.

Style: It's All About Looking Good

FORM VS. FUNCTION

Surfer style is mostly about comfort and functionality. You're looking for shorts with pockets for your keys and sweatshirts with hoods to keep you warm and dry when you get out of the surf. It's all about dressing for the elements. Even if it's warmer inland, it can be downright chilly at the beach, so pack layers. That way, you can strip down to a tank and shorts in the sunshine or warm up as it cools down in the evening with a cozy sweater or sweatshirt and pants. Check out Roxy, Delia's, Pac Sun, and Old Navy—surfer style is everywhere you turn these days! Think summer, sand, and sun, and you'll be dressing like a surfer girl before you know it.

SHOES THAT MAKE THE GIRL

Wear what you want, but every surfer girl needs a great pair of flip-flops, including a good pair that are waterproof. Get a pair that are all rubber or rubber and vinyl as opposed to those cute leather ones with the rhine-stones. Your feet will get very dirty with sand and tar, and you want to be able to hose everything down, including your shoes. Reef and Rainbow makes some quintessential surf-slipper options. When the weather turns cold, you may also want a pair of UGG boots. While UGGs have clearly gone in and out of fashion, they were invented by surfers for surfers. And while they aren't the most flattering shoe—trust me—put on a pair and you may never wear anything else again. It's like stepping into sunshine when you put them on your cold tootsies in the middle of winter.

PROTECT YOUR EYES

Unfortunately, you can't wear sunglasses while you are out in the water surfing; they won't stay on, even with a strap. But you are going to be spending a lot of time in the sun, so make sure to protect your eyes at least when you are on land. Onshore, those $5 sunglasses from the farmers' market are tempting, but make sure they have UV protection (your eye doctor's office can test your glasses for you if you are not sure). Wraparound sunglasses are best because they block the most sun, but whether square, round, or cat's-eye shaped, just remember to *wear your sunglasses*! Consider getting polarized lenses that cut glare, since the reflection off the water (or snow) is causing you to receive double UV exposure. If you are a contact wearer, some manufacturers have contacts that contain UV protection. Ask for them next time you are at the eye doctor's.

HINT Goggles aren't worn surfing simply because they come off when you get tumbled. However, you can wear your contacts surfing; just close your eyes when you hit the water.

HATS

Find yourself a cute summer hat that you love to wear that will protect the delicate skin on your face. Tightly woven, wide-brimmed hats are best, and darker colors are best for keeping out the sun's rays. If you choose to wear a baseball cap, make sure you have plenty of sunscreen on your neck, ears, nose, and chin. Although these caps are good for shading your eyes, that's about all they do. In the water you will sometimes notice people surfing while wearing hats that strap under their chins to protect their eyes and face from the sun. I won't lie: you won't look cool with one of those on. However, you will have the last laugh when you keep your stunning complexion as the rest of us get old and wrinkly.

PATRON SAINT OF SURFING

Surfers have adopted St. Christopher as their patron saint, and wearing his medallion around your neck is thought to protect you in rough seas. In the 1960s the medal was also synonymous with fleeting romance, so guys and girls exchanged them as a symbol of going steady. St. Christopher is most popular as the protector of travel, but he is also revered by surfers, mariners, ferrymen, and gardeners. Although it's not mentioned in the Bible, the story goes that the extremely buffed Christopher devoted his life to carrying people across a rough stream. One day a child appeared before him and asked to be carried across. The child was Jesus, and he rewarded Christopher's service by miraculously transforming his staff into a living tree. Wouldn't you know it, though, St. Christopher was decanonized during the late twentieth century. Surfers always seem to hang out with fringe characters.

CHAPTER VI

It's All About the ATTITUDE

BEING A SURFER GIRL has little to do with geography. Having the right attitude is more important than whether or not you can stand up on a wave. Although the following rules may be about surfing, you can apply them to any sport; they can also be incorporated into your everyday mind-set.

Surf with Aloha

If you are a beginner or even a veteran surfer, have the right attitude. It's all about having fun, communing with nature, and goofing around. Leave any grudges or bad attitudes at home and surf with aloha and peace.

Support Your Sisters

Give encouragement, share waves, and don't drop in on your sisters. We are the minority out there, so give a little love to the other chicks in the water. Give 'em a smile when they paddle out and a hoot when they catch a good wave. Compliment them. There is no greater buzz than someone telling you, "Nice ride."

Help Others

Once you have a clue about surfing, help those less fortunate than yourself. If you see a newbie who can't get through the white water, give her some love and show her how it's done. (Just make sure you know more than she does.) Sometimes giving an encouraging smile is enough.

Go for It

Nobody likes a lazy surfer. You are going to have to work really hard to learn to surf. You'll need to paddle your ass off, fall more times than you care to mention, and ingest tons of seawater. So really go for it when you are out there and make the most of every session. Everyone will respect a beginner who is working hard to become a better surfer, but there is nothing more frustrating than a beginner who is lounging around in the lineup and getting in people's way without so much as even attempting to catch a wave.

Don't Be a Priss

I am not saying don't be girly—wear pink, paint your toes, and don pigtails—but you are going to have to take some hard knocks out there and get a little dirty. You will have tar on your toes and sand in your hair. Your feet will get cut up and your knees will be bruised, but you will be having such a blast you won't have time to care.

Fear Factor

We don't have an appropriate English word, but surfing takes some *cojones* (that's "balls" for those not familiar with Spanish vernacular). I know, I know; we're girls and we don't have balls, but think of it as *chutzpah,* the Yiddish word meaning audacity and boldness. Even small surf can be intimidating. The ocean is unforgiving and you have to become familiar with it for your comfort level to go up. And when you are contending with other surfers and boards are flying at your head, your instincts may send you screaming to the shore. I don't mean to sound too Zen or anything, but overcoming fears in the ocean will help you step up to the plate in everything you do. Don't paddle out into head-high waves as a beginner, but get out there, grit your teeth, and paddle as hard as you can for that two-footer. Once you catch it, you will realize you can do just about anything.

Don't Leave Surf for Surf

A friend of mine gave me this piece of advice. If it's breaking where you are, there's no need to drive for hours to a spot that may or may not be good. Save your gas and energy for a day when your local break isn't producing any waves. Trust me, you will do a lot of driving around looking for surf.

You Should Have Been Here Yesterday

Surfers love to talk about good rides and great conditions, and I'm all for it, but don't be the girl who always seems to have it better than the rest. You know her; she's the one who always says, "It was epic yesterday," or "You should have been here earlier." Even if it was better two hours before your friend arrived, let her enjoy her time, too.

We Will Not Be Intimidated

Boys, or even naughty girls, may try to intimidate you out in the water. Poor sports may steal your waves, pick fights, and harass you. Don't let this spoil your session or your day. These silly people just aren't getting it. If someone gives you a hard enough time to get you out of the water, as my old coach said, "Laugh it off and come back strong tomorrow." Don't let anyone ruin your surfing experience; if you love it, no one can take that away from you. Just think, you've got a whole crew of surfing sisters to back you up.

Just One More Wave

Many a surfer has been late for work, school, dinner, or a date because of the "one more wave" rule. You're out there and decide you will just take one more wave before you come in. All of a sudden the conditions go totally flat, nada, nothing, not a wave for days. But you can't paddle in; that would be blasphemy. Finally, five, ten, twenty minutes later, on the horizon you see a dark spot, a wave coming your way. You paddle, catch it, ride it in, but it wasn't the perfect ride. So you paddle out again. Just one more wave.

CHAPTER VII

Surfing with the Boys

WHAT'S SO COOL ABOUT SURFING is that genderwise it's an equal opportunity sport. It takes strength, agility, and grace, but it's not necessarily easier for the boys than the girls. We may not have quite as much upper-body strength, our hips may be wider, and we have boobs that can make our balance and stance slightly different, but still, surfing for both sexes is basically the same. There are no restrictions; you alone determine how great a surfer you will be.

While the odds are changing, it's still about a one to four ratio of girls to guys in the water. More likely than not, when you paddle out, there are going to be more men in the lineup than women. Most of your encounters with the boys will be positive. For one, they are hot! Often my favorite part of my surf session is driving through the parking lot and checking them out (Whoops! Am I not supposed to say that?). Guys are great in that they will push you to challenge yourself. They may help you excel by pushing you to try moves and surf spots that you might not try on your own. Most guys are stoked to see girls out in the water. Girls are fun to look at, good to talk to, and often lighten the mood. Often, I am the only girl out with a group of my guy friends. I always think it's fun to hang out with the boys; you get to see what they really talk about. Mostly it's fantasy football, but every now and then you get real insight into their testosterone-filled world.

Learning from Your Boyfriend, Husband, or Significant Other

If you want to learn to surf, you may be a pretty competitive girl already, so perhaps it's not the best idea to have your boyfriend try to teach you. But if you are a great listener and your partner is the most sensitive, understanding guy in the world (or a surf instructor), go ahead and give it a whirl. Just don't blame me when it turns into a screaming match. I'm looking out for your relationship here! It might be better to spend a couple days at a surf school or camp before you paddle out with your man. It will be great to learn what he has to teach, but this way you will already have some good experience and safety rules under your belt so that the situation doesn't turn into a total catastrophe.

This goes for guys who are just friends as well. Guys are great and some can be good teachers, especially those who are trained and actually teach classes, but if a guy friend promises to take you out and gives you a 5'10" board and leaves you stranded with a "Have fun," he isn't someone you want to learn from. Be careful of letting a guy push you further than you want to go. Know your limits. Feel free to say, "This place is too hard," and call it a day. The ocean takes no prisoners, so don't go out into overhead conditions just to impress a guy when you are not ready. Most likely you will end up getting into trouble by embarrassing yourself or, worse, being injured.

Here's a very stereotypical look at the other types of guys you may find out in the water: the old-timers, the pros, the jerks, the kooks, and the grommets.

Old-timers

These guys have been surfing this break since before you were born. They look like your dad or even your granddad. Give these guys the respect they deserve. If you have questions, they're the ones to ask. They could probably give you an anecdote from that spot that happened back in 1959.

The Pros (Also Known as the Locals)

These guys have this spot dialed in. They surf here every day and aren't particularly worried about what you are up to. They will zip around you but are mostly harmless. These boys usually fall into the "don't bother me, I'm surfing" category. Best to save conversation with them until you are on the beach.

The Jerks

As a girl you get away with more, and guys may let you off the hook when you do something stupid. But boys will be boys, and some can be overly competitive and even mean out there. I've been yelled at, glared at, and run into. I've noticed that this behavior is usually exhibited by guys who are only mediocre surfers, so I guess they have some sort of inferiority complex. The good ones, at the worst, may get annoyed, but they seem to be able to sense your skill level and will know how to avoid you. Don't let the jerky guys (or girls) get you down. They are probably being jerks to everyone, and it's certainly not a reflection on you. Remember, everyone is allowed a chance to be a beginner.

Kooks

Kooks are surfers who think they can rip but can't, and they are only called kooks if they are on bad behavior. These guys are close cousins to the jerks, but they will usually leave you alone. They will steal your waves, however, and snake you without a word of encouragement. Don't worry, everyone else out there thinks they are kooks, too.

Grommets

Grommets are the surfers who sit on the inside and are usually under the age of fifteen. They will sit in front of you and catch all those late-breaking waves. Be careful of running into them, but these kids are quick and usually know how to stay out of your way. They are like dogs underfoot, cute but annoying. "Speed bumps" are their boogie-boarding cousins.

The Pickup

So what do you do if you like one of these surfer boys?

A lot of guys work under the no-socializing-in-the-water rule. If you are getting that vibe from a guy—that he takes his surf time very seriously—perhaps you should leave him alone until you are on land. Some guys will come up to you and ask, "Surf here often?" or ask about conditions (read Chapter XI: The Ocean and Surf Reports, and you will sound like a total water woman!); heck, yeah, if they are of interest to you, feel free to start up a conversation. If, however, you've got some guy squawking in your ear and you aren't feeling it, you can always say something like, "If you don't mind, I'm trying to focus" and then paddle away. Some guys won't really talk, but they'll want to impress you with their expertise. I always fall for the good surfers. Pull a great hang ten or an off-the-lip and my heart starts to flutter. Be prepared to impress those boys right back. Work on your skills. There is nothing sexier than a girl who can rip.

CHAPTER VIII

The Landlocked Girl

BEING A SURFER IS A STATE OF MIND. I say you don't need waves to be a surfer girl, just the right attitude. You can be a surfer whether you live in Honolulu, Hawaii, or Boise, Idaho, from coast to coast and everywhere in between. How can a girl keep her cool even when the waves are miles away? Just check out some of the following activities that will keep you ready, surfer girl, so that when you get the opportunity you are already halfway there.

Swim

Swimmers make the best surfers. Get in a pool or lake, whatever you've got. Goof around, swim laps, whatever. Get yourself totally comfortable in the water. Freestyle swimming is the best for surfing.

Balance Board

For fun in itself and great training get a balance board. Balance boards will get you ready for surfing and keep your stance in check—and they are a total blast. Made up of a large dowel and a mini board shaped like a surfboard, balance boards let you practice balancing, "walking your board," and goofing around. They are a tad pricey (Indo Boards, the leader in the area, cost around $100), but if you can't get to the waves, these can be a lot of fun, and if you are already a surfer, the balance board is great for core strength training. You can find these online or at your local surf shop.

You will notice a large warning label on the deck of a balance board that says USE AT YOUR OWN RISK. No kidding, I'd been surfing for years before I got on a balance board, and when I finally did, I wobbled, I bobbled, I looked like a total kook. To avoid flying off into your mom's glass coffee

table, start safely. If you have carpet in your house, practice on that; it will give you slightly more grip. Also, start somewhere where you can hold on to a doorjamb or something equally stable until you get the feeling of balancing. Be careful of practicing around anything breakable.

Start your practice by standing on the board with your feet on each end, knees bent, and weight kept over the center of the board. Then continue by rocking the board back and forth, lowering your weight up and down, hanging ten (standing with the toes of both feet hanging over the edge)—the tricks are limitless. A balance board will also help with your snowboarding and skateboarding skills.

Got Snow?

Snowboarding is the surfer girl's winter sport. If you are near mountains and have snow in the winter, consider taking up snowboarding. Although the two sports aren't totally alike, they share many similarities— especially the adrenaline rush, the fun, and the freedom. Slushing down the hill and carving turns will give you the same buzz that surfing does and will help you with your balance and stance. And just as in surfing, you will be in a gorgeous locale. The scenic beauty of the mountains will take your breath away.

Concrete Jungle

No waves or mountains? Consider skateboarding. Skateboarding isn't just for the boys. More and more girls are taking to the sport. New longboard skateboards give you the sensation of carving up a wave, and shorter boards let you perform countless tricks. It's just a concrete ocean, and shredding it up will help your balance skills and keep you in surfing form year-round.

Windsurfing

In case you have a body of water that doesn't produce waves, windsurfing might be for you. Windsurfing is like surfing but with a sail on your board, so instead of being propelled by waves, you are being transported by the wind. Balance and upper-body strength similar to surfing requirements are needed in windsurfing as well.

Kite Surfing

Kite surfing, a variation of windsurfing, is exploding on all bodies of water—rivers, lakes, and oceans. Kite surfing is a fusion of surfing, wakeboarding, and kite flying. Standing on a surfboardlike board with foot straps or bindings, kite surfers use the power of a large kite or parachute to harness the wind and propel them through the water. Don't live near the water? No problem. In the winter you can carve through the snow!

Wakeboarding

Got a lake and a fast boat? Wakeboarding is the latest evolution of water-skiing sports. It can be thought of as waterskiing on a small surfboard with footstraps (or boots similar to water-ski boots). The stance is partially or completely sideways just as it is in surfing. When the boat pulls you, it creates two waves as it displaces water, forming the wake. By steering the board, you can move outside the wake, then rapidly back in, hitting the wake and launching into the air. Or you can carve up and down the face of the wake to feel as if you are surfing!

Get Away from It All

Surfers love road trips and camping. Sometimes we must journey forth in search of good waves and small crowds. It's nice to find that little bit of solitude where you and your friends can feel as if you have the whole world to yourselves. Go camping with your friends, or take a road trip to a new location. Even if you can't hear the waves breaking from your campsite, you will have tapped into that independent surfer spirit.

Mental Vacay

If you can't physically get to surf, go there mentally. Watch surf videos and read surf magazines. Surf the Web and plan your next trip. How about taking a bath, reading your recent issue of *SG* magazine, lighting some plumeria-scented candles, and pretending you are in Hawaii?

Surf Decor

Decorate your room in a surf-inspired way that will keep you feeling like you are at the beach wherever you are. Take surf posters out of magazines, frame them, and then hang them on your wall (or for those with a slightly larger budget, hang painted beach scenes). Get tropics-inspired bedding or Hawaiian quilts. Hang a surfboard on your wall or even better, cut a skimboard in half and use it for cool shelves. Hawaiian kitsch can look surprisingly sophisticated when done right—hula girls and tiki lamps are fun for anyone's abode. Shells will make you feel beachy just about anywhere.

CHAPTER IX

Care and Grooming

SURFING MAY FEED YOUR SOUL, but sand, salt, and sun do a number on your hair and skin. Here are some après-surf tips that will help a girl keep tresses to toes in immaculate condition—and some health tips to cure what ails you.

Hair

Salt and sun will keep up your highlights year-round but, unfortunately, will also dry out your hair. Rinse your hair with fresh water as soon as you get out of the surf. Use a deep conditioner once a week to tame dried-out tresses. For those who don't want any lightening, use a spray-in conditioner for extra protection before you get in the water.

If you have long hair and you want to tie it back, a ponytail would seem the easiest way. But since your hair gets tugged around so much in the water, a ponytail can cause hairs to break around the band and cause frizzies and flyaways. My hairdresser recommends wearing braids because they cause less havoc for your hair, or tying it up in a bun.

HINT You can wear your hair down, but when you come up from under water, you'd be bummed if your hair was in your face or blocking your vision.

Skin

SUNSCREEN

I've said it before and will say it again, sunblock! Sunscreen is the only beauty product that can truthfully claim to prevent aging and wrinkles. Protection of the skin from sun exposure is required for all races of people, everywhere, and should be part of every skin-care program. Adolescents especially should be religious about using sunscreen because the teen years are when the most damage is likely to happen. Choose a broad-spectrum sunscreen with both UVA and UVB filters. You have more of a chance of getting burned on a cloudy day, so don't ever forget to cover up.

Studies show that most of us don't apply enough sunscreen to get adequate protection. You need an ounce of sunscreen lotion to protect the entire expanse of sun-exposed skin (to put it in terms we are familiar with, that's about a shot glass). Give sunscreen a good twenty minutes to bind with your skin before heading outdoors. Stash a tube of sunscreen in your beach bag and reapply every one to two hours as you sweat or wash off. If you're beach bound or playing sports, opt for a highly water-resistant formula. Studies show that the nose and ears are often missed when people apply sunscreen. Other forgotten zones include the backs of knees, hands, neck, and the tops of feet. What was once known as PTH (prime tanning hours), commonly 10:00 A.M. to 4:00 P.M., should now be known as "protect thy health." Try to avoid being in the sun during peak hours, but if you must be outdoors, use sun-protective accessories like hats and sunglasses; and seek the shade as much as possible.

SUNBURN

We aren't going to get sunburns, are we? We are going to be super careful and apply our sunscreen as mentioned above. You'll need to be especially careful if you are taking medications, since some react severely with sun exposure. Check for warnings and ask your doctor. Should you get a sunburn, however, some helpful remedies are listed below. (If you blister or develop a fever as a result of your burn, consult your doctor.)

ALOE VERA

If you did get a little too much sun, apply a soothing aloe gel. This natural moisturizer comes from the aloe vera plant and can be squeezed from its leaves. You can also purchase aloe vera creams and ointments that may include other moisturizers or treatments for dry or burned skin.

ANALGESICS

Analgesics (or painkillers) actually kill the pain of most sunburns for a time. One form, such as Lidocaine, is applied to the skin in the form of a spray or gelatinized rub. It is also frequently mixed with aloe vera. Use it sparingly because it can be absorbed by the skin and cause severe reactions. Aspirin or Motrin will also help decrease the inflammation and pain of sunburn. Topical cortisone cream will reduce pain, swelling, and redness. Start with over-the-counter strength cortisone, but if it doesn't get better or there is severe blistering, see a dermatologist.

VITAMINS

Vitamin E, an antioxidant, can be taken regularly as part of a daily vitamin and mineral supplement or applied as an ointment on sunburn. Vitamin C is another antioxidant that will help prevent severe damage from sunburn and shorten its effects. Selenium is a mineral that will help treat sunburn.

HINT Get your skin checked yearly by a dermatologist.

MOISTURIZER

Salt water can dehydrate your skin. A good daily moisturizer brings back moisture and helps prevent premature wrinkles and fine lines. Depending on your skin type, you will need to pick out the right moisturizer for you (dry, oily, or sensitive skin), and you may need different levels of moisture in summer as compared to the dry winter months. Choose a daytime moisturizer containing at least an SPF 30 sunscreen so that you are always protected. At night, a more intense moisturizer will help rebalance and normalize your skin as you sleep.

HINT Do you really need to wear makeup while surfing? I think not. Besides the fact that you are in water, and everything would wash off, your huge smile will be enough to get the boys' attention.

RASHES

If your skin gets red, itchy, or bumpy, you could have a rash. Minor allergic rashes are usually no big deal, but if it gets worse, is very itchy, or begins to spread, try an over-the-counter cortisone cream. When you wash the area, use clean water and stay away from soaps and lotions that may irritate the rash further. If this doesn't help, consult your dermatologist for sound advice.

HINT Keep your wet suit, bathing suit, rash guard, and board shorts clean and let them dry out fully between uses to decrease your chance of bacteria growth, which may cause a rash.

JUST SAY NO TO TANNING BEDS

Surfer girls don't fake bake. Dermatologists have warned all along that if your skin is tanned, your skin is damaged; ultraviolet light, whether it's from natural sunlight or a tanning bed, can lead to skin cancer.

But while tanning beds are off limits, if your tanning salon has spray-on mist tanners and you are feeling a little too winter white, go for it. Safe and UV free, this new high-tech treatment gives you a great-looking tan in minutes. With the push of a button, mist tanners spray a fine solution usually consisting of dihydroxyacetone (DHA), bronzer, moisturizer, and aloe. Expect treatments to cost around $20.

But remember, fake tans don't protect you from the sun. You will still need to use a daily sunscreen, and don't forget to reapply it!

SUNLESS-TANNING TIPS

Bottle tans are also good, but you get what you pay for, so read the labels carefully (look for products with DHA, which is better than carotene for a golden tan). And for goodness sake, don't turn yourself orange! Here are a couple of tips for you do-it-yourselfers:

DON'T OVERAPPLY

One application of tanner lasts for three or four days. If you keep adding layers, your skin will get darker and darker. The goal is a healthy glow; use too much and people may tease you for resembling a carrot.

EXFOLIATE AND MOISTURIZE

Avoid streaking and overaccumulation on the thicker, rougher skin of ankles and elbows by exfoliating first with a gentle body scrub. Removing dead cells will allow you to apply the product smoothly. Moisturize and then apply tanner mixed with even more moisturizer. Also, choose a cream or gel tanner that is tinted, rather than white or clear, so that you can see if you missed a spot.

BEWARE OF COLOR DYING YOUR HANDS

Wear latex gloves to apply the tanner so that it doesn't soak into your palms and get under your fingernails. If you must use bare hands, scrub your hands and nails well when you're done. You may end up getting residue on your clothes, so do the job at night, then wait at least twenty minutes before putting anything on. Wear something you don't care much about instead of your cutest bedtime outfit. You'll be tan by morning.

Heat Exhaustion/Heatstroke/Dehydration

Symptoms of heat exhaustion can include extreme fatigue, paleness, nausea, dizziness, lightheadedness, vomiting, and fainting. If you or someone you are with exhibits these conditions, stay in a cool shady environment, and if one is available, place a cool washcloth on the forehead or back of the neck. Hydrate with water and replace electrolytes by consuming a sports drink. If body temperature remains elevated even after treatment, it's best to consult a doctor for further information and instruction.

Heatstroke is a medical emergency and the most severe form of heat-related illness. Unlike other forms of heat illness, heatstroke is not necessarily caused by exercise or exertion. High temperatures, lack of body fluids, and overexposure to the elements can all bring about heatstroke. Symptoms can include flushed skin, a body temperature of 106 degrees or higher, seizures, headache, and unconsciousness. A person with heatstroke may feel cool and clammy and will not be sweating. Anyone exhibiting the signs and symptoms of heatstroke should be rushed to the nearest hospital.

To avoid dehydration and these heat-related disorders, follow these simple steps: Keep your body well hydrated. Sports drinks and/or water are the best choices; drink plenty before, during, and after activities or exposure to the sun. As a surfer you will most likely be cooling yourself off in the water, but beware of overdoing it. On especially hot days or in hot environments, it is advisable to taper back a bit until your body has adjusted to the heat. If you feel yourself getting warm or lightheaded, it's best to take a time-out and rest in the shade.

Swimmer's Ear

Swimmer's ear is an infection of the ear canal caused when the acid content of the ear changes and bacteria penetrate the skin. It can make the ear itch or become red and inflamed enough that even touching the ear is very painful. In a worst-case scenario, you may see pus drain from the ear.

If you develop swimmer's ear, apply a few drops of white vinegar diluted equally with water into the ear. Avoid putting objects in the ear (for example, fingers or cotton swabs) that may scratch the ear canal and cause further infection. It is not necessary to thoroughly dry your ears after swimming or surfing; just let them air dry. If irritation persists or ears continue to feel clogged, consult your health-care provider.

Surfer's Ear (We Wanted Our Own Ear Condition)

Surfer's ear (also known as exostosis) is a condition in which excessive bone growth occurs inside the ear canal when cold water or cold air repeatedly enters the ear. Surfer's ear, which is six times as common in cold-water surfers as warm-water surfers, can eventually cause a partial or even complete blockage of the ear canal resulting in a loss of hearing. In severe cases, surfer's ear is treated with an operation in which the surgeon drills the bone down. Since I can barely describe it without becoming weak in the knees, let me mention how to avoid it: wear a hood or earplugs to lessen the impact of the cold water and, perhaps, decrease your chances of getting surfer's ear.

Pinkeye/Conjunctivitis

There is a possibility that you could get pinkeye from bacteria in the water. Symptoms include redness and discharge (usually in the morning) that makes the eyes feel like they are stuck together. You will need to get antibiotic eye drops or ointment prescribed by your doctor. Do not use medication prescribed for someone else or for a previous infection because these may be contaminated. Wash your pillowcases and bedding, and clean sink areas well so that you don't keep reinfecting yourself. Try not to touch your eyes; pinkeye can be highly contagious.

Drainage

After a good surf your nose will sporadically drain and a river of water will flow out (usually when you bend over) because of all that water getting into your nasal passages during wipeouts. Murphy's Law says it will drain right when you are talking to the cute guy you are trying to get a date with. It's something every good surfer experiences, however, so you need not be embarrassed. Usually, it makes for a good talking point and proves you surfed hard!

Feet and Toes

Sprained ankles, stubbed toes, and bruises are your feet's main concerns when you're surfing. The answer is never to jump feet first off your board. Water depths fluctuate, and while you may think you are in three feet of water, you may only be in inches. Jumping off your board can cause a rude awakening. If you are surfing over reefs or rocks, be especially careful about putting your feet down on them or pushing off against them. As well as potentially hurting ocean life, you put yourself at risk of stepping on a sea urchin or other sharp, prickly object.

HINT Pedicures won't last long for the surfer girl; and since the sand is so abrasive, it will take the shine off your perfectly painted toes. For a long-lasting pedicure, wearing booties will keep your polish in place.

Staph Infection

Cuts from coral or reef rash (getting raked across the reef and cutting yourself up in the process) could result in a bacterial infection known as staph. Be sure to clean out any cuts you have sustained while surfing with rubbing alcohol or an antibacterial ointment like Bacitracin. See a doctor if you have a wound that becomes infected or doesn't heal normally.

First Aid

You will get cuts and bruises while surfing. Take proper care of them. Make sure to clean out your cuts with hydrogen peroxide or antibiotics, because there are tons of bacteria in the ocean. As for bruises, try icing them down. You will look and feel kind of like a kid again with black and blue knees, but heck, it's worth it. You will also notice bruises on your ribs and hips where they stick out and rub against the board. This is normal and there is not much to do about it. Wearing a wet suit will help a bit by giving you a little cushioning.

WARNING Be wary of going into the water after a recent rain. Runoff and debris from city streets and sewers will have made their way into the ocean. And you don't want to be swallowing any of that water because it contains bacteria that could make you sick. Lay off for a couple of days until bacteria levels have dropped (check with Surfrider Foundation's Web site for updates and beach closures).

Stomach Illness

If you experience severe stomach cramps, vomiting, or diarrhea that you think might have come from polluted water caused by runoff, be sure to see your doctor right away. Sadly, because of pollution, there are lots of nasties in the water, including fecal matter, E. Coli, and other forms of bacteria, which are all potential for disease. As a precaution, make sure you are up to date on your vaccines (including hepatitis A, which can be transmitted through fecal matter). This supergross information should only encourage you to become an environmental activist!!

Malaria

Malaria is prevalent in many tropical areas. It's a serious, sometimes fatal, disease caused by a parasite that is transmitted though infected mosquitoes. Flulike symptoms include chills, muscle aches, nausea, and vomiting. If you know you are going to an infected area, get an antimalarial prescription from your doctor. If you think you may have malaria, consult your doctor immediately.

Just for the Ladies—Period

Your period should not get in the way of your surfing experience. I wouldn't recommend wearing a pad (it will just fill up with water and be really uncomfortable), but you can wear a tampon to feel secure.

According to some shark experts, menstrual blood (and urine) almost certainly can be detected by a shark. Have there been any documented cases? No. However, if you are surfing in a known shark-infested area, and it is that time of month and you know your flow might be a little more than your tampon can handle, perhaps you should think twice about surfing.

Yeast Infection

Walking around in a wet swimsuit or wet suit could cause a yeast infection. A yeast infection is cause by an imbalance of candida (a yeast or fungus that is normally found in moderate levels in the body). You will know you have one if you get itchy down below and/or there is excessive discharge from your vagina. Yeast infections are common and easily treated with over-the-counter antifungal medication or one prescribed by a doctor.

To avoid getting a yeast infection, change out of your wet suit or bathing suit into breathable cotton clothing as soon as possible after you're out of the water and dry off well. Also, avoid clothing that fits too tightly, since it may trap moisture. Keep it clean, cool, and dry down there and you should be fine.

In case of this or anything unusual, consult your gynecologist.

Gotta Go?

Peeing in your wet suit is not recommended (hello, did you just read about the sharks?!) because urine will rot the neoprene, but sometimes it is a must because getting out of the water, getting off your wet suit, and even finding a bathroom is a total haze. If you ever see me floating around off my board, you will know what I am up to.

If you *really* have to go, for the sake of the rest of us, please find a bathroom.

Pregnancy

If you are recently pregnant, let's wait to learn how to surf until after delivery, m'kay? However, if you are already a surf goddess who has become pregnant, can you strut your stuff out in the water? Although light activity and exercise are suggested, my ob/gyn doesn't suggest surfing because the risk of falling or getting hit with a board is just too great. And lying on your belly would be just plain uncomfortable. Also, as a woman's belly gets bigger, her center of gravity shifts, which might cause you to lose balance more easily. If you can't stay away, opt for knee paddling and go easy. You have your baby to worry about now.

Don't be silly ladies; this book is merely a point of reference. If you get a real injury—are hit with a board, cut by a skeg, banged on the reef, bitten by something big, or see something weird on your skin—go to the doctor immediately!

CHAPTER X

Conditioning

THE ONLY WAY TO IMPROVE your surfing skills is to surf! But there are a few things you can do to increase endurance, surf stronger, and keep yourself injury free. In the beginning you will spend 99 percent of your time paddling and about 1 percent actually riding the wave. So get in shape, girl. You will need to!

Those of you who don't live near the beach can get on board with the nutrition advice and workout activities listed below. That way you will be in surfer-girl shape when you take off for that great surf camp vacation!

Nutrition

WATER

One of the biggest problems you can run into while surfing is dehydration. Drink water and plenty of it. Forget soda (although Gatorade or rehydration drinks are good) and stay away from those caffeine-energy drinks, like Red Bull—the caffeine will dehydrate you. If you can't steer clear of Starbucks when you get out of the cold water, at least supplement it with a glass of water. *Water,* you hear me? Drink some before you go out in the surf and lots after you come in.

HEALTHY FOODS

As a surfer girl, you need to eat like an athlete. Cut back on the fast food and think whole foods. Stay away from overly processed foods and go for more natural choices like fruit, nuts, and whole grain breads. We've all heard about balance and moderation  and, no joke, these are the keys to a healthy diet. Be careful of portion size. It's okay to indulge in a small ice-cream sundae every now and then; just don't impress your friends by eating an entire banana split solo!

PROTEIN AND CALCIUM

Make sure you are getting enough protein to build your muscles. Eat lean cuts of meat, poultry, fish, and shellfish for your protein fix. If you don't eat meat, you can get protein from tofu, veggie burgers, beans, and nuts. Avoid fatty cuts of meat, bacon, sausage, and fried foods.

Do eat low-fat milks and cheeses, which are a great source of calcium. Avoid whole milk and whole-milk products. Eggs are great and full of protein; just be careful not to lose all that goodness by preparing them with excess butter and oil.

CARBOHYDRATES

For energy, choose vitamin-rich carbohydrates, such as oatmeal, whole grain bread, and brown rice. Don't gorge on chips and cookies. And don't go overboard

on refined flour and rice products, from which most of the nutrients have been stripped. Use whole wheat flour. It will give you longer lasting energy than white flour. Read labels: if you're eating a whole wheat product, then whole wheat flour should be listed as one of the first three ingredients.

HINT Eat your fruits and veggies. They are all good for you. However, try to avoid eating veggies cooked with excessive butter, oil, or cheese.

FATS

All fats aren't necessarily bad. Avocados (great for skin and shiny hair); olives; nuts like almonds, walnuts, pecans, sunflower seeds, and pumpkin seeds; and fatty fish like salmon are great for you. Avoid foods containing excessive butter, lard, and shortening.

And for dessert, lay off sweets like candy bars, too many cookies or cakes, doughnuts, and ice cream. Instead, opt for low-fat frozen yogurt, fruit popsicles, sherbet, or sugar-free Jell-O. (But don't look to me on this one; I am a chocolate chip cookie junkie!)

SOME GREAT SNACK IDEAS

Celery with peanut butter (make sure to buy all-natural peanut butter that doesn't contain sugar or hydrogenated oils)

Apples and cheese (Parmesan, string cheese, and mozzarella are all good choices and are lower in fat than some of their cousins, like Cheddar, Swiss, Jack, and Brie)

Yogurt with granola (make sure the granola doesn't contain a lot of coconut or hydrogenated oil)

Power bars, whole grain cereal bars, or
   low-fat granola bars (always better
   than a candy bar)
Carrots with a low-fat ranch dip
Fresh fruit smoothie—blend a banana and some strawberries
   with low-fat yogurt and milk—yum!
Hard-boiled egg
Trail mix
Popcorn (either air-popped or low-fat)

If you're hungry, eat a small snack before your surfing session. Too much might slow you down (and lying on your stomach with a full belly might make you a little queasy), and then eat a nice meal or healthy snack when you get out to help rebuild fatigued muscles.

HINT The old wives' tale about waiting an hour after eating before swimming is not altogether true. Although muscle cramps may occur in the legs, feet, or hands while surfing, they have little or no relation to how much you have just eaten. The American Red Cross suggests, "In general, you do not have to wait an hour after eating before you may be able to swim safely. However, if you have had a large meal, it is wise to let digestion get started before doing strenuous activities such as swimming." Something to take into consideration after a picnic lunch on the beach.

"SURF'S UP" COOKIES

This slightly healthy alternative offers a little more nutrition than a regular chocolate chip cookie and is sure to satiate your sweet tooth after a hard day of surfing! It isn't your typical cookie, but you may find it totally addicting.

1/3 cup butter, softened

2/3 cup brown sugar

1/4 teaspoon ground cinnamon

1/4 teaspoon baking soda

1 egg, beaten

1/2 cup applesauce

1 cup all-purpose flour

1/4 cup whole wheat flour (or if you don't have whole wheat flour,

1 1/4 cups all-purpose flour is fine)

1 1/4 cups rolled oats

1/2 cup chocolate chips or carob chips

1/2 cup chopped walnuts

Preheat the oven to 375 degrees.

Cream the butter and brown sugar together in a large bowl. Mix in the cinnamon and baking soda. Stir in the egg and applesauce, then add the flour and oats a little bit at a time. Mix in the chocolate chips and walnuts.

Drop rounded teaspoonfuls of dough onto an ungreased cookie sheet. Bake for 8 to 10 minutes.

Makes about three dozen

Exercise

Surfing is great exercise. It is amazing for upper-body endurance, and you will find (especially at the beginning) that surfing can be a good workout, since you spend most of your time paddling around. The better you get, sadly, the less of an aerobic activity it becomes. To be a great surfer you will need to supplement your surfing with some cardio, strength, and flexibility training.

Flexibility Training

If you're younger, you may not fully understand the soreness and stiffness we older ladies feel after a day of heavy activity. But it is a good habit for old and young alike to work on flexibility. For those of us who have it, let's hold on to it, and those of us who have lost it (I swear I could do the splits when I was younger), let's get it back. Flexibility is the key to injury prevention. It helps balance muscle groups that might be overused during exercise or physical activity.

Static stretching involves a slow and controlled elongation of the muscle through the full range of motion, and it is held for ten to thirty seconds in the farthest comfortable position (without pain). Stretching also improves muscular balance and posture and increases blood supply and nutrients to joints. (It increases tissue temperature, which in turn increases circulation and nutrient transport.) This allows greater elasticity of surrounding tissues and increases performance.

Prior to stretching, you should begin with a simple low-intensity warm-up (such as walking) for five to ten minutes. Overall flexibility is key, but your arms, shoulders, and back get the most use surfing. Start each of the following stretches slowly, exhaling as you gently stretch each muscle group.

STRETCHES
CROSSED-ARM STRETCH

This is my favorite surfer stretch. Start with your arms out straight in front of you; bend elbows to 90 degrees so that your fingers point toward the sky and your upper arms are parallel to the floor. Cross one arm above the other so the elbow is nestled in the crease of the opposite arm. Wrap arms around each other so that your palms are touching and lift your elbows to get a great upper-back stretch. Switch sides. Yum!

SIMPLE TWIST

Lie flat on your back with your arms straight out to the sides at shoulder level; bend your knees and keep your feet flat on the floor. Slowly drop your knees to one side while turning your head the opposite way. Try to keep your shoulders on the floor. Hold the stretch and come back to the starting position. Switch sides.

TRICEPS STRETCH

Raise your arms overhead, bend your right arm, and place your palm flat on your back. With your left hand, gently pull your elbow to the left to get a nice triceps stretch. Be sure to keep your head in a neutral position and shoulders relaxed. Hold and then switch sides.

CHEST/SHOULDER/BACK STRETCH

Clasp hands together and bring your arms up in front of you, parallel to the floor. Pull your hands forward and simultaneously push your upper back away from your hands (as if someone were pulling your hands and your back in opposite directions). You should feel a nice stretch between your shoulder blades. Also try this to the back. Clasp hands together behind you. Raise your arms while keeping them straight to feel the stretch in you shoulders (you can also incorporate this with a forward bend).

NECK STRETCHES

Drop your head forward and roll it back and forth, from your left to right sides—slow and deep so you can feel the stretch in your neck muscles.

SEATED HAMSTRING STRETCH

Sit on the ground with your legs straight out in front of you. Bend your right leg and place your right foot flat against your left inner thigh. Bend from the waist while keeping your back straight and slowly move your hands forward along your left leg toward your toes. Your left leg should remain straight with your toes pointed toward the ceiling. Grasp your thigh, calf, or toes, depending on your flexibility. Change sides.

Also try forward bends by leaning over straight legs with your feet together or in a wide stance, hands on (or reaching toward) the floor.

QUADRICEPS STRETCH

Start in a standing position. While holding a stationary object for balance, bend your right leg behind and bring your foot up toward your butt so your knee is pointing toward the floor. With one hand, grasp your ankle or foot and pull it in toward your buttocks until you feel a good stretch in your quad (be careful not to take this stretch into your knee). Keep your back straight and do not allow the knee to drift forward or in back of the standing leg. Change sides.

SWIMMING

The best way to train to be a surfer is by swimming. Hop into a lap pool and swim! That's all there is to it. Familiarizing yourself with the water and becoming a strong swimmer are key to good surfing. You never know when your leash may snap and you will have to swim to shore.

Once you have mastered the basics, try working up to this swim set: using freestyle (or free), which is the stroke most similar to paddling a surfboard, start off at an easy pace for 200 yards. An Olympic-sized pool is 50 meters long and 25 meters wide, so that's four lengths if the lanes are set up for a long course or eight lengths if the pool is set up for a short course. When you've completed the laps, take some breaths on the edge of the pool as needed. Then try 50 yards at a faster, harder rate. Rest again if you need to. Then try another 50 at the same pace, or push it a little harder. Take another breather, and then go for another 100 yards. Your choice: either push hard or you can start to take it down a notch. Finish up with a 200-yard cooldown, any stroke you like. Aside from the noted rests, take breaks whenever you need to. As you build up endurance, swim additional yards.

HINT To perfect your freestyle stroke, remember to keep yourself in a straight line. Don't tilt your head up; it will sink the rest of your body. When you breathe, turn your head directly to the side, making sure to keep one ear in the water. Use nice long strokes and don't forget to kick with your entire leg. It should feel as if you are gliding through the water.

Also try extending the periods you swim underwater to prepare yourself for the dreaded "hold-down" (when the broken waves hold you down under the water). The more relaxed you stay, the longer you will be able to stay under (don't let this freak you out though; beginner breaks rarely, if ever, hold you down for any extended length of time).

The more you swim, the more you will improve your endurance and strength, getting you ready to surf!

CARDIO ACTIVITY

The more cardio activity you do out of the water, the more endurance you will have in the water. You will be able to stay out longer and surf better and stronger. The idea of cardio activity is to get your heart rate up. There are fancy equations you can do, but I figure if you can feel your heart working and you get slightly flushed, you are working hard enough. If you start to feel dizzy, for goodness sake, back off!

If you live in a climate where you can do outdoor activities, walking or running are ideal. Hiking up a beautiful trail is great for body and soul. If you live in climates slightly less hospitable, join a gym. There you can use the treadmill or try the Stairmaster or elliptical machine to vary your program.

Try to do at least twenty to thirty minutes of cardio activity two to three times a week.

STRENGTH TRAINING

Weight training is great, especially for us women because it will help fight osteoporosis (bone loss). Do exercises on a balance board or ball to increase your workout. They incorporate core muscles along with the primary muscle group you're targeting. Doubling up on your strength training this way is good for all-over toning and conditioning, which will help your balance when you're surfing.

There are many exercises you can do at the gym with weights. Ask certified trainers to help you and tell them you are training for surfing. Here are a couple of exercises you can do wherever you are. Try doing three sets of ten to fifteen each.

PUSH-UPS

These are the all-time best for surfing. Depending on your upper-body strength level, you can try either a traditional push-up or, if that is too much, try them with your knees on the floor at all times. Begin on your hands and knees (or balls of your feet if you are more advanced) with hands slightly more than shoulder width apart in front of you, fingers facing forward. Move into a plank position. While keeping your body as straight as possible and trying not to let your butt or back droop, bend elbows and lower torso toward the floor until elbows are bent at about 90 degrees. Be sure to keep abs and torso tight. Using chest muscles and triceps, straighten your arms to bring your torso back to the starting position.

TRICEPS DIP

This is the opposite of a push-up. Stand in front of a stable chair or bench, with your back to it as if you're about to sit down. Bend knees and lower hips so you can place hands at the edge of the seat. Fingers should be pointing forward with arms straight. Walk feet forward and with feet flat on the floor and torso erect, bend arms to 90 degrees, then straighten.

PULL-UPS

Pull-ups are great for your shoulders, lats, and biceps. Grasp a bar (you can often find pull-up bars in parks or playgrounds) slightly wider than shoulder width apart and pull yourself up so your chin is just above the bar. In a controlled manner, lower yourself back down. It's okay if you can only do one or none when you start. If you're unable to do any, try this: keep your legs crossed at the ankles and bent in a 90-degree angle while a partner holds your feet and helps lift you into position.

LUNGES

Begin with feet hip width apart, chest lifted, and abs tight. Step forward with your right leg so that your right foot is flat on the floor and you're standing on the ball of your left foot. With torso erect, lower yourself so that your right thigh is perpendicular to the floor and your leg forms a right angle. Make sure your knee is right over your ankle—pushing it too far forward or back could damage your knee. Your left leg should also be bent at a right angle with your knee directly below your hip. Return to the standing position using your glutes and thighs. Then switch legs. When you can do these easily, incorporate weights or try doing lunges while you walk.

CRUNCHES

Lie with your back on the floor, legs bent, feet on the floor, hands behind your head, and elbows pointed away from you. While pulling your belly button toward the floor, lift yourself up until you feel your stomach muscles engage; then lower yourself slowly. Keep your head in a neutral position and don't place your chin on your chest. To make sure you don't crunch your neck, my trainer used to suggest keeping your eyes on the corner of the room where the ceiling meets the wall.

OBLIQUE CRUNCHES

These are similar to crunches, but they're done to each side of your body. Lie on your back with knees bent and extend your right arm to the side at shoulder level; place your left hand behind your head. Pull abs in and lift head, neck, and shoulders off the floor. Rotate left elbow toward the right knee, keeping hips on the floor. (Think of bringing your chest to your knee, not your head to your knee.) Return to the starting position.

YOGA

I am convinced that yoga is the be-all and end-all to better surfing, since it's all about balance (ideal for improving your board work), strength (don't tell me it's not hard to do those *chaturangas*), flexibility (key to injury prevention), and focus (paying attention out in the water is key to safe surfing). Despite what you may think, yoga is about much more than sitting around meditating. And you don't need to be flexible to do it (sadly, I have never in my life been able to touch my toes, and I still do yoga a couple times a week).

Although yoga is a five-thousand-year-old scientific technique for spiritual development (yoga is a Sanskrit word meaning "union," the goal being the unification of body, mind, and spirit), it can be whatever you want it to be: an intense workout, a relaxing meditation, and/or a spiritual experience.

Check out local yoga studios or see if your gym offers classes. There are some great videos that you can use at home if you can't get to a yoga studio. Peggy Hall's video series *Yoga for Surfers* is a fine way to start. She targets specific muscles and balance poses that are key to surfing.

SUN SALUTATIONS

Trying to describe a sun salutation on paper is almost as futile as teaching you how to surf with a book alone. However, in case you can't wait to rent a video or take a class here goes . . .

A sun salutation *(surya namaskar)* is a flowing series of postures. Each movement should be coordinated with the breath.

MOUNTAIN POSE

Start with feet together and planted firmly on the floor; stand as tall as you can, arms relaxed at your sides.

ARMS OVERHEAD

Take in a deep breath and bring your arms out to the sides and up over your head, keeping them straight until finally touching palms.

HEAD TO KNEES

Exhaling, dive down into a forward bend so that you're touching your knees, toes, or floor, depending on your flexibility.

HEART FORWARD

Still in a forward bend, inhale and stretch your heart forward as far as you can while extending your spine.

PLANK

Hands on the floor, exhale and either jump or walk your feet back into a plank position (top of a push-up). Hold the position and inhale.

CHATURANGA

With an exhale, lower down as if you were lowering from a push-up, but with your elbows tight by your sides.

(continues)

(continued)

UPWARD DOG

Inhale and push your head and chest forward and up, pushing arms straight into the floor so that your back is arched and your legs are straight out behind you, toes pointed. You will be in somewhat of an L-shape, head at the top, hips on the floor, and feet out behind you. Ideally, weight should only be on your hands and the tops of your feet (knees should not be touching the floor).

DOWNWARD DOG

From here, exhale and push back into downward dog. Push straight back without moving your hands, and roll your toes over so you are on the balls of your feet. Lift your hips up to the sky and straighten your legs and arms. Think of your body as a right angle with your feet and arms firmly on the floor bearing your weight. Lift up from the hips toward the ceiling and push your heels toward the floor. Take five breaths in this position.

HEAD TO KNEES

Exhale and jump or step your feet forward to meet your hands. Straighten your legs. You are now back in a forward bend.

ARMS OVERHEAD

With a flat back, inhale and raise your torso and arms back up and overhead.

MOUNTAIN POSE

Bring arms down into prayer pose (palms touching in front of your heart). Start over.

Namaste.

PILATES

Long used as a training method by dancers and gymnasts, Pilates is a great training program for surfers. Gaining popularity because you can now perform it on a mat on the floor, as opposed to on the Reformer (a specialized machine that you could use only in a studio), Pilates focuses on building a healthy, injury-free body by encouraging controlled and concentrated movement. It improves strength, flexibility, balance, control, and muscular symmetry by working core stabilizing muscles. The exercises promote toned, elongated muscles and a strong body core. You can find Pilates mat videos online and in many bookstores.

CHAPTER XI

The Ocean and Surf Reports

THE OCEAN IS A LIVING, breathing force, and there is no better thrill than diving right in. Here is a little bit of oceanography for you to impress your friends with (it should also help make you a better surfer). Be sure to read this section. It's good for you, like eating broccoli, and you'll know more than most of the boys out in the water.

Waves

To answer the question *Why do waves break?* you would need a degree in mathematics and physics. Terms such as *stability criteria* and *nonlinearity* give me the heebie-jeebies, but here it is in the simplest terms. It is information you should actually know.

Wind and storms way out in the ocean create the waves we surf. Waves can travel vast distances across the ocean without losing much energy. When they finally reach our beach, they crash and break, releasing energy. This happens when they enter water that is approximately 1.3 times as deep as the wave is high (a 3-foot wave would break in approximately 4 feet of water). At this depth, the part of the wave that is at the seafloor slows down (through friction with the bottom) while the crest (top) keeps moving. As the water gets shallower, the bottom of the wave keeps slowing down while the crest moves on unaffected. The wave breaks when the face, or front of the wave, becomes too steep and the crest begins to separate from the wave below it.

The size and shape of breaking waves result from the steepness and shape of the seafloor. If the bottom slopes gently, the result will be a slow, crumbly wave. On the other hand, if the bottom rises very steeply, the wave encounters the bottom only at the last minute. The result is that the bottom of the wave slows down very quickly while the crest goes speeding by, resulting in a faster, hollower wave. Sometimes the result is an open-air space in the wave known as a tube by surfers (Pipeline is an example of this kind of wave).

Whew! Check out the movie *North Shore* for an explanation from Chandler if this is still confusing.

HINT Wave measurements are arbitrary. Here on the mainland, we measure the face or front of a wave, but Hawaiians measure wave height from the back. So while we say a head-high wave is about 6 feet, they call a head-high wave 3 to 4 feet. In Europe they measure the front of the wave but use meters, so head high is about 2 meters (1 meter = 3.28 feet). Be careful when you are traveling to a new location to be sure to stay in your own comfort zone no matter what measurements are being used.

Shore Break

As surfers, we are hoping to surf waves that break far enough from the shore to give us time to ride them in. But even these spots will have shore break (waves that break right on shore in shallow water). The force of shore-break waves can throw unsuspecting swimmers and surfers down and is responsible for many neck and back injuries. Be careful entering and exiting the ocean because even small shore break can throw you down, which is terribly embarrassing and sometimes painful—especially when you have a big board thrashing around next to you.

Swells

A swell is a long ocean wave (caused by a storm way out at sea) that moves continuously without breaking. The size of the swell depends on the intensity of the wind within the storm, the distance the wind blows across the water (called fetch), and the length of time it blows. There are two kinds of swells that will affect your surfing conditions.

Wind swells are generated by local winds within a few hundred miles of the coast. As a result, the swell periods are short, and the waves tend to stack up on each other in messy arrangements. To a surfer these kinds of swells will produce waves that come in quickly, one wave right after another, and they usually don't have much "umph" to them. You may paddle for a wind swell, only to have it dissipate as it goes by.

Groundswells are generated by winds much farther away. These waves have left the storm area and organized themselves into lines of swell. As they travel, they generate greater length and speed. The results are waves that come into shore powerfully and evenly, to the delight of surfers.

WARNING You may be surprised, while your break might be totally mellow in summer, come winter, storm surge, strong currents, and constantly changing bottom conditions can turn your spot into an advanced surf mecca that may be over your head (literally and figuratively).

Rip Currents

A rip current (aka rip tide or rip) is a section where the ocean current moves away from the beach (all that water heading toward the beach in waves needs to escape somehow, right?). A rip current can usually be recognized by its choppy water and foamy, brown color as the water mixes with the sand being picked up from the ocean floor. However, some rip currents lack contrasting color and are harder to spot. They can range in size and shape, expand up to hundreds of yards in length, and can even migrate up and down the beach.

The best way to avoid getting stuck in a rip current is to have strong swimming skills and to understand how a rip current works. Most of the time it is very difficult to swim directly against the current. If you are being pulled away from shore in a rip current, do not fight against the current but swim parallel to shore until you are clear of the outgoing flow and then swim in. Do not panic. The current will pull you out, but it will not pull you under.

Tides

The ocean is constantly swishing back and forth with the help of the earth's rotation and the gravitational pull of the moon and sun on the earth. Tides create the natural ebb and flow of the ocean. The tide usually changes from low to high (or high to low) approximately every six hours. Tides become more extreme when there is a full or new moon, and they can also be exaggerated by large surf and storm surge. The range of the tide can vary.

In Hawaii, the tide may rise or fall only a few feet every six hours, but in Southern California, it can be as great as 8 feet. Spots in Europe and the Pacific Northwest can have tide swings as big as 25 feet in a six-hour period! As you become familiar with breaks, you will find that some work in relation to a high or a low tide.

Remember to be careful during low tide, since rocks and coral, which are usually sufficiently under water when the water levels are high, can be exposed.

Winds

Winds are usually classified as offshore and onshore.

Offshore winds blow from the land toward the ocean. These are what surfers are after. **Onshore winds** are winds that blow from the ocean toward the shore and generally make for poor surfing conditions because they create bumps and chop on the water (check nearby flags, smokestacks, or palm trees to see which way they're blowing). You can still surf during light onshore winds, but as they become stronger they will completely ruin the waves.

You may be asking yourself why surfers get up so darn early. The main reason is that early morning is when the ocean is the calmest. The wind is usually still or offshore at dawn and turns onshore mid to late morning. The water will get choppy once the wind picks up (that's why you don't see many surfers out in the afternoon). The wind dies down toward evening as the air cools inland and flows offshore.

Ocean Life

The ocean is teeming with life. Seeing dolphins act as if they're at Sea World, performing tricks and jumps right in front of your eyes out in the open ocean, makes a girl want to run right out and join Heal the Bay. Tons of marine life is out there swimming around you. Depending on your area, you may see dolphins, seals, tropical fish, sea turtles, or otters. The ocean is a magical place and most of the sea life is lovely to look at and won't harm you. There are some ocean inhabitants, however, that have the potential to make for an unpleasant surfing experience.

Here are some creatures to take into consideration:

SEA URCHINS
Roughly eight hundred species of sea urchins can be found in various marine environments throughout the world, particularly in areas of sea

grass beds and coral reefs. These creatures, which can grow to be three feet in diameter, are housed in a "test," which is covered with sharp spines with barbed ends. The spines might contain venom and have the potential to bring infections. Sea urchins are often stepped on or run into by the unsuspecting surfer. Most cases of infection cause mild to severe pain for a few hours, but some infections last for months, especially if pieces of spines are left in the wound. Removal of spines should be done surgically or with extreme caution so as not to break them further. To treat a sea urchin injury: the protruding spines should be carefully removed, the wound should be soaked in hot water (110 to 115 degrees) to break down toxins, and analgesics should be used to relieve the pain. Consult a doctor if you have an imbedded spine, suffer a delayed reaction, or show signs of an infection. If the spine impinges on a joint space, tendon, or nerve, a surgical consultation is required.

To prevent stepping on a sea urchin, resist pushing off of coral reefs with your feet. Sea urchins offer a surfer just another reason to wear booties.

CORAL

Coral is actually a colony of tiny animals called polyps, which are related to and look like sea anemones. The reason coral is hard and a danger to surfers is that coral secretes a stony cup of limestone around itself as a skeleton. The polyps divide as they grow and form coral colonies. As the colonies build up on top of one another, they gradually form a sharp coral reef. If you step on it, you'll get pieces of it embedded in your feet, and if you fall into it, it can cause serious injury.

Coral cuts (also known as reef rash) must be thoroughly cleaned with fresh water. First, apply and then remove adhesive tape to pull out small, hard-to-reach pieces. Scrub the area to ensure that there are no embedded coral particles. Finally, flush the wound with a hydrogen peroxide/water solution, then rinse again with water. Use an antibiotic ointment and keep the wound clean, dry, and properly bandaged. If the wound shows any sign of infection, you should see your doctor.

STINGRAYS

The stingray, a flat-bodied fish with a long whiplike tail armed with one or more serrated, venomous spines, is common in shallow sandy areas. The stingray inflicts wounds by lashing out with its tail. Remember, when entering the ocean with a sandy bottom, it is a good idea to shuffle your feet so you don't step on any stingrays. They aren't aggressive; they lie on or near the bottom, submerged in the sand, and usually only sting when people step on them. Their sting can cause very deep lacerations, profuse bleeding, and serious swelling. If you get stung, clean the wound with mild soap and water; then soak your foot in hot water (110 to 115 degrees for up to two hours—after two hours heat is ineffective) until the pain lessens, and clean again to prevent infection. If barbs are stuck in your foot or anything seems unusual, see your doctor.

JELLYFISH

In most locations, jellyfish stings are the most common marine injury to surfers. Jellyfish are just what their name implies. They are invertebrate marine animals that look a lot like, well, jelly. Typically, jellyfish catch their prey with the aid of stinging cells located in the tentacles; many jellyfish can cause irritating or even dangerous stings to humans. The severity of a jellyfish sting depends on the species and the amount of contact with the tentacles. To treat a jellyfish sting, you should pour either vinegar or baking soda on the wound to disarm the nematocysts (stinging capsules), which inject the poison or the venom. If these substances are not available, seawater can be used to rinse off the tentacles (hee hee, urine works too!). Fresh water, alcohol, ammonia, or bleach should never be applied to a jellyfish sting because these cause the nematocysts to discharge their venom.

Similar stings can come from the Portuguese man-of-war. In the case of a sting, remove all tentacles carefully with gloved hands or a stick. Rinse with salt water or fresh water and apply ice to alleviate pain. *Do not use vinegar in this case because it can cause the nematocysts to fire.*

SEABATHER'S ERUPTION (AKA SEA LICE)

Sea lice isn't actually lice at all. It is a sting by the juvenile stage of the *Linuche unguiculata* jellyfish. It occurs sporadically from March to August, peaking in May in warm waters off the shores of North Carolina down to Florida, Texas, the Caribbean, and Fiji.

Symptoms can last up to two weeks and include itching, welts or blotches, fever, nausea, and blisters. The affected area is usually concentrated under bathing suits where the larvae become trapped.

Experts say the best way to avoid this sting is to listen to reports and observe daily posted beach messages; don't go in the water if they're expected. Others suggest wearing a waterproof moisturizer such as zinc oxide or thick layers of Vaseline all over exposed skin to block the stings. It couldn't hurt to try Safe Sea lotion, which claims to protect you from jellyfish sting (and contains SPF).

If you get stung, over-the-counter cortisone cream or an oral antihistamine may help ease the symptoms. And make sure to wash your swimsuit with detergent. In the case of severe reactions, call your physician.

RED TIDE

The name *red tide* comes from the reddish-brown color reflected from the enormous blooms created by these organisms. Red tides are natural conditions caused by high concentrations of phytoplankton (such as dinoflagellates and diatoms).

Going out during a red tide bloom is generally safe for surfers. At worst, it might cause eye and throat irritation. If you choose to go surfing in red tide conditions, make sure to rinse off with clean water as soon as you get out of the water.

Don't eat locally caught fish during a red tide bloom because neurotoxins from the red tide can accumulate in fish, mammals, and invertebrates (such as clams), and there is always the potential that they will pass on disease.

KELP

Kelp ranges in size from minute plants invisible to the human eye to the giant kelp that can reach up to 200 feet. It's mostly found in cooler water along the California coast. Why do surfers like kelp? Because the choppy water created by onshore winds gets blocked by the kelp bed's canopy zones on the surface of the water. Theoretically, this keeps the water on the shore side of the kelp glassy and smooth (although depending on the weather, this isn't always the case). Kelp is generally harmless, but your leash or skeg may get stuck on it while you are paddling or taking off. It could slow you down or make you miss a wave.

WHAT YOU ARE REALLY WONDERING ABOUT . . .

Yes, there are sharks. Yes, we are surfing in their playground. Yes, there have been highly publicized shark attacks in recent years. There are about four hundred known species of sharks, but only thirty species are realistically dangerous to humans and about a dozen are reported to be especially aggressive and dangerous. Great whites, tiger sharks, and bull sharks are the most dangerous to humans. Sharks are certainly a concern, especially in their habitats (Florida, South Africa, Hawaii, and California are all hot zones), but they shouldn't keep you from surfing. (More realistic concerns include getting whacked in the head with a board.) Shark interactions with humans are primarily based on mistaken identity or curiosity, and you are more likely to die under a falling vending machine than from a shark attack. In the case of a shark sighting at your local break, however, steer clear. No reason to tempt fate.

REDUCE, REUSE, RECYCLE

The ocean gives us the gift of surfing every day, and all it asks in return is that we keep it clean. Ocean conservation philanthropies come out with depressing facts about pollution in our waters every year. Below are some stats from the Surfrider Foundation:

Eco Facts

- Everything that enters a storm drain goes directly to the ocean (litter, used oil, antifreeze, sewage, toxic chemicals, pesticides, and so on).
- Dumping one quart of motor oil down a storm drain contaminates 250,000 gallons of water.
- Urban storm water is one of the top three sources of pollution of our nation's rivers, lakes, oceans, and estuaries.
- Three and a quarter million tons of oil enter the oceans of the world each year.
- In the United States, sewage treatment plants dump 5.9 trillion gallons of waste water into coastal waters each year.
- More than 60 percent of the world's coral reefs are threatened by pollution, sedimentation, and overharvesting from the curio and aquarium trade.
- Fourteen billion pounds of garbage are dumped into the world's oceans every year, most of it in the Northern Hemisphere.

The average citizen *can* make a difference. Write, fax, call, or e-mail your congressional representative, senator, and the president to let them know that you support stronger environmental laws.

SURFRIDER FOUNDATION'S LIST OF
TWENTY THINGS YOU CAN DO:

1. GET YOUR MIND OUT OF THE GUTTER
Sweep your driveways and sidewalks. Put trash in the can instead of the gutter. Use your lawn clippings to fertilize your lawn.

2. PULL YOUR OWN WEEDS
The fewer herbicides and pesticides you spray, the fewer you will swim in on the weekend.

3. PLANT, DON'T PAVE
Let the runoff water soak into the ground. Landscaping looks better and creates oxygen.

4. SCOOP THE POOP
Unless you like to swim in animal poop, make sure you and your neighbors pick up the droppings.

5. REPORT FULL CATCH BASINS
Departments of public works should clean full storm sewers.

6. FIX YOUR CAR LEAKS
More oil enters the beach from urban runoff than from tanker spills. If your car drips, the oil will find its way to the ocean.

7. DON'T BE A DRIP
Low-flow showerheads and toilets and drip irrigation conserve water. Repair any leaks.

8. MINIMIZE WATER LOSS
Water lawns in the morning or evenings. Water deeply and less often for happier plants.

9. USE NONTOXICS
Vinegar and baking soda clean very well. Buy ecosensitive products now available on the market.

10. OIL'S WELL THAT ENDS WELL

Recycle your motor oil at a garage. Don't dump it into a storm drain.

11. RECYCLE—ONCE IS NOT ENOUGH

Recycle reusable materials. Call 1-800-RECYCLE for drop-off locations.

12. BE AWARE OF STORM DRAINS

The trash and toxins that are dumped on the street run straight to the beaches. If we reduce the amount of slime that goes into our storm drains, our coastal waters will be protected.

13. QUIT USING STYROFOAM

The coffee generation brings its own mugs. Let the shop owners who use Styrofoam know you disapprove.

14. PEOPLE CAUSE POLLUTION; PEOPLE CAN STOP IT

Next time you see some trash, pick it up.

15. JOIN A LOCAL ACTION GROUP; GET INVOLVED

If you're not part of the solution, you're part of the problem. Check the facts and vote. One more voice does make a difference.

16. COVER YOUR TRAILS

Take household hazardous materials and containers to a local collection program for disposal.

17. CONSIDER, CONTROL, CONSERVE

Recycle reusable materials. Throw litter into trash cans and keep cans tightly covered to prevent foraging by animals.

18. DON'T WATER THE DRIVEWAY

It won't grow. All that water washes to the beach.

19. TALK AROUND TOWN

Because most people don't realize they are contributing to nonpoint source pollution, spread the word and get your neighbors and coworkers involved.

20. HOLD ON TO YOUR BUTTS

The beach is not an ashtray.

The good news is that conditions are improving. Activist groups such as the Surfrider Foundation, Heal the Bay, Oceana, The Ocean Conservancy, and the World Wildlife Foundation (WWF) have improved the state of our oceans and beaches. They focus on protecting marine life through cleanup and education programs and serve as watchdogs over polluters and developers whose actions would continue to destroy our great oceans. Become involved, whether it's by joining an environmental group, recycling, or just picking up a piece of trash on the beach. You can make a difference!

Surf Reports

Surf reports are great. They provide advance information so that you don't load up your car, drive miles to the beach, and end up in flat conditions, or, as a beginner, you don't show up at a beach where the waves are double overhead. There are plenty of available surf reports on the Internet, which are easily accessible and free to use. Type in "surf report" and your location in an Internet search engine and you will be surprised how many sites you can find. Ask around—your local surf or dive shop may have a number to dial for daily surf reports as well.

WAVE HEIGHT

The first thing you will see is the height of the wave. The report might read 1–2 or 3–4+. As mentioned earlier, areas measure the face of the wave (Hawaii being the exception). A measurement of 1 to 2 feet is usually knee-to-waist height, and it's a great beginner wave. A measurement of 3 to 4 is waist to shoulder, and 5+ is head high or more. That last measurement is fun stuff as you become a better surfer, but it's not a good idea to try to learn on that kind of day. Remember you are paddling on your stomach, so even a 1- to 2-foot wave will look big from your vantage point.

CONDITIONS

Conditions usually read (plus or minus) Poor, Fair, Good. They refer to the shape of the wave. Poor usually means "mushy" (the waves are crumbly and don't have much umpf to them) or "closed out" (the entire wave breaks all at one time, leaving you nowhere to ride). Fair means you will probably get a couple of workable shoulders that give you room to maneuver and take off. When conditions are good, the waves are great and clean—head out!

TIDES

The report will also tell you when high tide and low tide are for that day. For example, in Southern California, expect to see numbers that range anywhere from about −1 foot to 6 feet. With a lower tide, more rocks and reef can be exposed. With higher tides, certain breaks may flatten out and become mushy. You will need to know what works best for your break. You can find this out by word of mouth, or some Web sites may tell you. If you read that there is a low of −0.2 feet at 8:30 A.M., and you know your spot is better on a medium tide, you might want to wait to go out until 9:30 or 10:00 A.M.

HINT Tides can be predicted years into the future. You can look up tide tables on the Internet, or you can get an entire year's worth of tide predictions from tide books, which are found at your local surf shop or anywhere that sells sailing or fishing equipment. They are usually free, and it's a good idea to pick up a couple and keep them in your car or with your surf stuff.

DIRECTION

A surf report will usually tell you which direction a swell is coming from and at which degrees. Northern Hemisphere storms, which cause northern swells, usually happen during the months of October through April. Southern Hemisphere storms are more common in May through September. Aha! It's winter during this time in these regions. Ask around to find out what swell direction your surf spot picks up.

BUOYS

When you get a little more sophisticated, you can check online for data about your local buoy. Buoys are an early warning system for swells. They float out in the ocean (60 miles, 200 miles, etc., from shore), and they record the height, direction, and interval of the swells hitting them. First you will need to know what swell your break picks up. Does it break on a south, north, east, or west swell? A buoy will tell you what direction the swell is coming from and the swell height (not the same as the ultimate wave height, but they are related). Although this usually takes a bit more guesswork, they can be a great predictor of the waves to come.

CHAPTER XII

History

WHERE DID SURFING COME FROM? Surfing has been around since before written records, and do you want to hear something cool? Women were always a part of it. While women did go through some lean times when surfing wasn't thought to be feminine, and some female surfers had to face more adversity than others, there have always been women riding waves.

Many women have contributed to shaping the history of surfing, and the following pages contain some of the highlights and milestones. You may know something about surfing history, but this is *her*story.

He'e Nalu

Centuries ago, surfing was born in the oceans on and near Hawaii, where it was common for as many women as men to be in the water. Although gender didn't seem to segregate surfers in ancient Hawaii, surfing, or *he'e nalu* (wave sliding) as it's called in Hawaiian, was mainly reserved for royalty. Commoners got their chance, too—just not at the same time or at the best breaks.

During this time it was known full well that if a man and woman happened to ride the same wave together, custom allowed certain intimacies when they returned to the beach. Wahoo! Courting rituals were also carried out in the surf, when a man or woman tried to woo and win a mate according to his or her performance on the waves.

PRE-1700s Pele, goddess of Volcanoes, was also known to surf, taught by the shark god Kamohoali'i. Pele in turn taught her sister, starting a great tradition of women's surfing!

1700s

The first written account of surfing was by Lieutenant James King in 1779 from the "Journal of Captain King, Cook's Voyages," shortly after the death of Captain Cook. The account is amazing to read by today's standards: "But a diversion the most common is upon the water, where there is a very great sea, and surf breaking on the shore. The men, sometimes 20 or 30, go without the swell of the surf, and lay themselves flat upon an oval piece of plank about their size and breadth, they keep their legs close on top of it, and their arms are used to guide the plank, they wait the time of the greatest swell that sets on shore, and altogether push forward with their arms to keep on its top, it sends them in with a most astonishing velocity, and the great art is to guide the plank so as always to keep it in a proper direction on the top of the swell, and as it alters its direct."

1800s

The 1800s were the dark ages of surfing. With the arrival of Captain Cook's men, disease spread and nearly decimated the Hawaiian population. Puritanical New England missionaries came to Hawaii and declared surfing a heathen sport—they weren't big fans of nudity and gender equality. By the beginning of the 1900s, surfing had just about died out except for a handful of surfers in Hawaii who were mainly men. Women were relegated back home to cook, clean, and look after the kids. Harrumph!

After a trip to Hawaii, Mark Twain tells a surf story in his 1872 book, *Roughing It*. "I tried surf-bathing once, subsequently, but made a failure of it. I got the board placed right and at the right moment, too; but missed the connection myself. The board struck the shore in three-quarters of a second, without any cargo, and I struck the bottom about the same time, with a couple of barrels of water in me."

1900s

In the early 1900s, as Hawaii became a more and more popular tourist destination, surfing regained its place in the sun in large part because of the Waikiki Beach boys. These local boys would take tourists out to surf the waves on surfboards and outrigger canoes and at night entertain them by singing and playing ukuleles. One of the most well known of the group was Duke Kahanamoku, who in 1912 won five medals in swimming at the Olympics held in Sweden. Thought to be the father of modern surfing, Duke popularized surfing with his highly publicized exhibitions around the world. Duke was also a founding member of the Hui Nalu (gathering surf) Club, officially formed in 1911 to promote surfing among Hawaiians. The club immediately sparked a friendly rivalry with the Outrigger Canoe Club, founded in 1908. Two of the Hui Nalu members were excellent female surfers—Mildred "Ladybird" Turner and Josephine "Jo" Pratt, who was known to be the best female surfer in the Islands from 1909 to 1911.

1907 Surfing was officially introduced to California by George Freeth, an Irish-Hawaiian surfer who was touted as the "man who could walk on water." Freeth was brought to Redondo Beach by Henry Huntington (the legendary land baron who built the Pacific Electric Railway) in the hopes of selling beach property to the crowds that would ride his railway down to catch a glimpse of Freeth surfing.

1914

At the age of fifteen, a woman named Isabel Letham became the first Australian to ride a surfboard. On December 23, 1914, Isabel rode tandem with Duke Kahanamoku when he introduced Australians to surfing at Sydney's Freshwater Beach. Isabel was hooked and continued to surf and swim the rest of her life. She went on to earn herself a place in the Australian Surfing Hall of Fame for her contributions and encouragement to women in surfing.

Weighty Boards

In the 1930s it seems that most women were content to sit on the beach or ride tandem with their boyfriends, mainly because surfboards were so incredibly heavy back then; they probably weighed as much or more than the girls riding them! Surfboards were made of pure wood, and few women could carry them—and they were a hazard to deal with out in the ocean. One noted California girl who overcame this difficulty was Mary Ann Hawkins, acclaimed as one of the greatest female surfers of the first half of this century; she was a graceful surfer as well as an excellent waterwoman.

1950 Joe Quigg, a famous surfboard shaper, introduced a new light-weight balsa board, also known as a girl board, to some of the women of Malibu.

Gidget

The surfing world would change forever after Kathy Kohner bought her first surfboard for $35 at Malibu's Surfrider Beach. Kathy told her father about her adventures with Malibu locals Mickey Dora, Mike Doyle, Terry

Tracy, and Bill Johnson (who provided Kathy's nickname Gidget because they said she looked like a girl midget). In 1957, Kathy's dad Frederick Kohner wrote the novel *Gidget* about his spunky daughter and her friends at the beach. All of America discovered surfing in 1959, when Sandra Dee portrayed Gidget in the first of three movies, and they came to the beach in hordes. In 1965, *Gidget* was turned into a television series starring Sally Field in the lead role.

The Women of the 1960s and 1970s

At the age of twenty-nine, Marge Calhoun's husband gave her one of Joe Quigg's new lightweight "girl" surfboards for Christmas, and a couple years later the California girl won the women's division of the 1958 Makaha International surf contest held on Oahu's West Shore. She attended the event with her friend Eve Fletcher (who had learned to surf only a year before). The two women spent a month surfing the waves of Hawaii and living out of a paneled van. Marge and her two daughters, Candy and Robin, both surfers as well, were thought to be the epitome of the California surfer girl throughout the early 1960s.

In 1959, Linda Benson, who learned to surf by standing on shore and waiting for the boys' surfboards to wash up (they didn't use leashes back then), won the first West Coast Surfing Championship at Huntington Beach at the age of fifteen. This talented goofy footer from California went on to win the Makaha International the same year. A couple of days after the Makaha contest, Linda went out and became the first woman to ride the big waves at Waimea Bay. She won the West Coast Championship again in 1960 and 1961 and won the United States Surfing Championship in 1964 and 1968.

1964 Linda Merrill, a goofy footer from Oceanside, California, was the first woman featured on the cover of *Surfer* magazine.

Joyce Hoffman won the World Surfing Championship held in Lima, Peru, in 1965. At just nineteen years of age, Joyce became the best-known female surfer of the 1960s. She was featured in teen magazines and *Vogue,* and was on the cover of *Life* magazine. Joyce went on to win the World Championship again in 1966 and was honored as one of the original eight inductees into the International Surfing Hall of Fame, which pays tribute to the many individuals who made surfing what it is today.

1968 Joyce Hoffman became the first woman to ride the powerful barreling waves at Pipeline, on Oahu's North Shore.

The year 1967 was the beginning of the shortboard revolution, when boards went from longboards (9 feet or more) to shortboards (approximately $6\frac{1}{2}$ feet) and the weight of the older heavy boards dropped nearly in half. The first woman to make use of these smaller, lighter boards was Margo Godfrey, who beat out Joyce Hoffman for the world title in 1968. Margo was a new breed of female surfer. Known as "the girl who surfed like a guy," she was more radical than the women before her and won four world titles: 1968, 1977, 1980, and 1981.

Late 1970s

Hawaii's number-one woman amateur surfer for five years, Rell Sunn embodied the aloha spirit and became known as the Queen of Makaha. In 1977, Rell Sunn founded Makaha's annual Menehune Contest, where young boys and girls compete in bodyboarding, longboarding, and short-boarding. Rell suffered from breast cancer, which took her life in 1998 at the age of forty-seven. There is a wonderful documentary celebrating her life called *Heart of the Sea.*

Jericho Poppler, the number-two ranked surfer in the world in 1979, was also a feminist and an activist. She was a cofounder of the Women's

International Surfing Association and Women's Professional Surfing, and later she became a founding member of the Surfrider Foundation and other environmental philanthropies.

ORGANIZATIONS

Various organizations have come and gone throughout women's surfing history. In 1975, the first Women's International Surfing Association contest was held at Malibu. (WISA was founded by Mary Setterholm, Jericho Poppler, Shannon Aikman, and Mary Lou Drummy to help address gender equality.) But in 1977, when newly formed International Professional Surfing (IPS) incorporated a women's tour, the WISA had difficulty staying afloat. The IPS's mission was to link together the different surfing events around the world in order to rank surfers and produce year-end champions. In 1982, with backing from Ocean Pacific, the ASP (Association of Surfing Professionals) replaced the IPS as the governing body of professional surfing. Although the ASP is still the main governing body, other women's groups have formed to fight for wave time, better conditions (women's heats are usually held in the afternoon, when wave conditions aren't as good), and media coverage. In 1981 Jericho Poppler, Rell Sun, Margo Oberg, and friends set up the short-lived organization Women's Professional Surfing (WPS). Almost all the female pro surfers were members the group, but it never gained much ground and closed its doors in 1986. In 1999, Rochelle Ballard and others founded the group International Women's Surfing (IWS) as a nonprofit organization with goals for increasing the value of the women's pro tour, specifically by creating a series of women-only events that could secure their own sponsorship dollars and media coverage.

Women of the 1980s and 1990s

In 1984, at the age of fifteen, Frieda Zamba, from Daytona Beach, Florida, shocked the competition by becoming the youngest woman to win an ASP world title. Zamba was later coached by her husband, local pro Flea Shaw. As a team they were unstoppable, and Frieda won four world titles. Wendy Botha, from South Africa, and Frieda battled it out over the next couple of years, and in 1987, Wendy won the first of her four world titles.

Pauline Menczer, from Australia, won the World Pro Tour at Sunset Beach on the North Shore of Hawaii in 1993. She gained the world title not only by battling the waves but also by waging a war with her body: she was suffering from rheumatoid arthritis.

In 1990, Quicksilver launched its sister company, Roxy. Named after founder Alan Green's daughter, Roxy brings surf style inland to any girl feeling the surfer spirit. Roxy was one of the first surf lines to recognize that women wanted the same kind of style and performance in their athletic gear as men. They started off with swimwear and boardshorts that were stylish as well as functional, and now they have a full line of surf gear, snow gear, clothing, and shoes. Other surf manufacturers have followed suit: Billabong, Rip Curl, Hurley, and O'Neill all have women's and girl's lines of surf gear and surf-inspired clothing.

Lisa Andersen ran away from her Florida home at the age of sixteen to surf at Huntington Beach. She left a note saying she was leaving to become the women's world surfing champion. When she got to California, she racked up thirty National Scholastic Surfing Association awards and then went pro. In 1987 she won the ASP Women's Rookie of the Year award. In 1994, after giving birth to her first child, Lisa fulfilled her wish and won the first of four consecutive world titles and was the featured on the cover of *Surfer* magazine. The cover read "Lisa Anderson Surfs Better Than You."

The Media

The media has taken surfing to its heart and tried to cash in on its lifestyle and cachet. Lots of movies and TV shows have glorified the surfer life. *Point Break* was released in 1991 and featured Keanu Reeves as an FBI agent who goes undercover as a surfer to catch a ring of bank robbers. More recently, in 2002, Universal Pictures released the feature film *Blue Crush,* about a young woman's quest to win the Pipeline Masters. The world was reintroduced to the surfer girl. And in 2003, television finally figured out just how popular surfing had become. That summer, MTV aired *Surf Girls*, a reality series where fourteen surfer girls compete for pro status, and the WB aired *Boarding House: North Shore,* which follows a household of surfers on the North Shore of Oahu during the coveted Vans Triple Crown of surfing. Surfers like Holly Beck, Veronica Kay, Chelsea Georgeson, Mary Osborne, and Molly Miller became household names.

The Women of Today

Layne Beachley, from Manly Beach, Australia, won the first of six world titles in 1998. Arguably the most well-known female surfer today, Layne's been dominating the competition for years and has used her success and the media to help introduce surfing to more and more women. Coached by former boyfriend and big-wave surfer Ken Bradshaw, Layne began towing into 25-foot waves and has become known as one of the few female big-wave riders.

1999 Sarah Gerhardt charged the big waves at Maverick's and became the first woman to ride the giant and dangerous waves of Half Moon Bay.

Popular surfer Rochelle Ballard, from Hawaii, has yet to win a world title, but that doesn't seem to be slowing her down any. She won the first of three Surfer Poll awards in 2000 because of her gutsy surfing and unbelievable tube time. She's been featured in many surf videos, including *Modus Mix* and *A Girls's Surf Addiction,* and was Kate Bosworth's stunt double in the feature film *Blue Crush.* Her training camp, the Rochelle Ballard Surf Camp for Chicks Who Rip, helps coach young surfer girls and inspires them to follow their dreams.

Keala Kennelly is not your ordinary female surfer. The goofy footer from Hawaii defies the stereotypes with her pierced tongue and passion for DJing, and she surfs hard. She was ranked number two in the world in 2003. Keala specializes in aerials (launching off the wave into the air and landing back on the wave) and barrel riding (riding inside the tube of the wave) and has won the Teahupoo event four times.

2002 Duke Kahanamoku was the first surfer featured on a U.S. postage stamp.

Look out for Holly Beck, Chelsea Georgeson, Sophia Mulanovich, Megan Abubo, Bethany Hamilton (who inspired the world with her spirit and surf stoke after she lost an arm to a shark attack while surfing), and others who have raised the bar of women's surfing and heightened its profile worldwide. These girls rip, shred, and dominate the competition, male or female.

Make some history yourself and get out there!

CHAPTER XIII

Surf Spots

HERE ARE SOME GREAT BEGINNER SPOTS where you can practice your paddling, turtle roll, and getting up without being harassed, yelled at, or beaten up. Watch out for other beginners though; chances are it'll be a little like bumper cars on a crowded day. Almost all the spots I chose have, within walking distance, surf shops where you can rent a board or sign up for a lesson. Look for spots with names like Sandy Beach; skip spots called Boneyard or Killer's.

I apologize to the locals and regulars in advance for the hordes of young women who might be hitting these spots. But you've got it great, so why not share some of your stoke with them? Newbies, remember to mind your p's and q's and give respect to get respect.

Mainland United States

CARDIFF STATE BEACH, CARDIFF, CALIFORNIA—Located between San Diego and Encinitas, Cardiff State Beach has a gently sloping sandy beach. Good surf at the spot will last longer than at the surrounding beaches because offshore kelp beds and high cliffs keep it protected from the wind. You can often find rental boards right on the beach. Lifeguards are normally on duty.

COROLLA, OUTER BANKS, NORTH CAROLINA—The north end of the Outer Banks offers gentle waves that are terrific for learning. Corolla, with about twenty-five miles of surfable sandbars, has a great entry-level surf break during the summertime. Because there are so many sandbar breaks, everyone can really spread out. There is plenty of public access to the beach and a local surf shop offers rental boards and lessons. (From **Kitty Hawk** to **Nags Head,** ask the locals about similar gentle breaks and surf shops.)

COWELL'S, SANTA CRUZ, CALIFORNIA—A great place to start out if you're new to the sport, Cowell's offers long, gentle waves for longboarding. It's generally understood that Cowell's is the spot for beginning surfers, so the scene in the water is crowded yet generally polite. It's easily accessed by stairs off of West Cliff Drive or by paddling out from the beach north of the wharf. Surf shops are located nearby, and there is an equipment truck parked on the beach all summer and year-round on weekends. (Down the coast a bit **Pleasure Point** is a good spot, too, but board rentals are a bit more of a hike—about three blocks away.)

DITCH PLAINS, MONTAUK, LONG ISLAND, NEW YORK—Ditch Plains is the most consistent wave on Long Island. It is perfect for beginners and longboarders, but it can be totally packed with surfers. The rental surf shop is about a mile away, so be prepared to get your board there either in or on top of your car, although parking at the beach is relatively easy.

FIRST STREET JETTY, VIRGINIA BEACH, VIRGINIA—The First Street Jetty is where it all happens in Virginia Beach. The rock jetty traps sand and forms what is often the best, and only, setup in town. Everywhere else can be a lake, but the jetty will usually muster a surfable wave. Lessons and surf camps usually take place here, but the closest surf shop that rents boards is about fifteen blocks away.

ISLA BLANCA BEACH PARK, SOUTH PADRE ISLAND, TEXAS—The water is a different color—the locals call it South Padre green—and the sand is nice and soft. It's a great place to go for good, fun surf—no bothersome marine life, no rocks, and a friendly local vibe. Head out by the jetties if you want an easy paddle out. There is a surf shop and a school on the island for rental equipment and lessons.

LA JOLLA SHORES, LA JOLLA, CALIFORNIA—Located just north of San Diego, this is the location of the extremely popular all-women's surf school Surf Diva. There is a gentle beach break and although it's crowded, everyone expects beginners, so it's low on attitude. You can rent boards on the beach, and about a block away there is a surf shop that rents equipment.

LINDA MAR, PACIFICA, CALIFORNIA—Located off Highway 1, just after the light at Crespi Avenue, Linda Mar's parking area entrance is on the right (just before Taco Bell). It has a fun beach break and it's a decent place to learn. Be careful; this spot can have big, gnarly waves in winter and during large swells. If you are a newbie, only go out on days when the waves are under waist high. The surf shop in the mall, just south of the parking lot, will rent you a board.

SHEPHERD PARK, COCOA BEACH, FLORIDA—Located on a barrier island on Florida's central east coast, Cocoa Beach is the hometown of Kelly Slater—so it's gotta be good, right? Because of its constant flow of solid ocean waves, Cocoa Beach attracts surf enthusiasts from all over the world. Ron Jon Surf Shop, a block from the beach, is open twenty-four hours a day (why?) and rents boards cheap! Most spots around Cocoa Beach offer good beginner waves, but Shepherd Park is where lessons are held, and it's within walking distance of rental surf shops.

SUNSET, LOS ANGELES/MALIBU, CALIFORNIA—Sunset is probably one of the best beginning spots in the Los Angeles area. It has a soft rolling wave, but it only breaks on a low to mid tide. I suggest entering from the south side on the "beach" instead of coming down the cliff or stairs. Sunset is located on Pacific Coast Highway just south of Gladstone's restaurant. You will need to bring your own board to this spot because there aren't any rentals nearby.

WATER PARKS

You don't even need to live near the ocean to go surfing.

Water parks around the world are implementing the FlowRider. FlowRider is a surfing platform on which riders maneuver their uniquely shaped boards on a continuous wave. The water rushes toward you as you surf in place. At the time of publication, the following water parks in the United States house a FlowRider where you can actually stand up:

Kalahari Indoor Water Park, Wisconsin Dells, Wisconsin

Wave House, Mission Beach's Belmont Park, San Diego, California

Others that offer a FlowRider where you can boogieboard or drop knee (kneeling stance with one knee down) are

Hyland Hills Water World, Denver, Colorado

Lake Lanier Islands Resort, Lake Lanier Islands, Georgia

Mitchell Pool, Great Falls, Montana

Paramount's Kings Island, Kings Island, Cincinnati, Ohio

Pharaoh's Lost Kingdom, Redlands, California

Schlitterbahn Beach Waterpark, South Padre Island, Texas

Schlitterbahn Waterpark Resort, New Braunfels, Texas

Six Flags Hurricane Harbor, Arlington, Texas

Water Mania Water Theme Park, Kissimmee, Florida

The Wave, Vista, California

HINT From personal experience, I recommend that you wear a rash-guard or wet suit over your bathing suit on the FlowRider, as water rushing at you at 25 mph tends to lead to overexposure (pulling your swimsuit in directions it should not go!).

Hawaii

You probably think of Hawaii as the world's surf mecca. Huge swells can hit the north shores in winter, giving surfers the opportunity to compete for cash, titles, and bragging rights. The west and south coasts are mellower and offer some great spots for beginners. Here are a couple places where you can head out.

BREAKWALL, LAHAINA, MAUI—On a good day, Breakwall offers up a good, long ride from a left-hand point break. On a normal day you'll find a decent crowd but not much in the way of localism. There is a coral bottom, so be careful of jumping off feet first and try to fall flat during wipe-outs. Loads of surf schools offer lessons here, and they're located right on the beach and across the street.

COVE PARK, KIHEI, MAUI—Kama'ole I, II, and III Beach Parks (the Kams) form a necklace around the town of Kihei. At Kam I the waters are calm, the sand is soft, and the beach slopes gradually into the water. Surfing instruction is often available at Cove Park at the extreme north end of the beach, and the gentle waves are great for beginners. It's relatively easy to park, and just across the street from the break is a surf shop that rents boards.

KAHALU'U BEACH PARK, BIG ISLAND—Just south of Kona, this is one of the only spots on the Big Island where you can easily rent a board at the surf shop just across the street from the break. The surf shop also offers lessons. Street parking is easy. Just look for St. Peter's Catholic Church and a small crescent of black sand beach.

POIPU BEACH PARK, POIPU, KAUAI—Located on the south side of the island, Poipu Beach is fronted by Poipu Beach Park and a few of the resorts. It was recently named America's Best Beach by the Travel Channel, ranking top among ten "best" beaches selected nationwide. Surf schools and board rentals are located right on the beach.

WAIKIKI BEACH, OAHU, HAWAII—This all-time best beginner break is located on the south shore of Oahu. This is the most well-known beginner surf spot for a reason: it offers unbelievably perfect, gentle rolling waves. Even though the crowds here are out of control, it is well worth a paddle out. You can rent boards right on the beach for about $20 an hour. Lessons are also offered.

International

BIARRITZ, FRANCE—This vibrant cosmopolitan town along France's northern coast also has killer surf. Surfing in France started in Biarritz, and surfers come from all over the world to ride the waves. There are surf shops around town that rent boards and offer lessons.

BYRON BAY, AUSTRALIA—This is the undisputed learn-to-surf capital of Australia, thanks to the winning combination of consistently pleasant weather, warm water, and beautiful beaches protected from big swells by Cape Byron. Head to **Clarks Beach, Main Beach,** or **Belongil** for beginner-friendly waves. Many surf shops in the area offer rental boards and lessons.

FISTRAL BEACH, NEWQUAY, ENGLAND—The infamous Fistral Beach is Britain's premier surfing beach and home to the UK's major surfing competitions and the International ASP event. Fistral is renowned for its quality and consistent waves. Lessons are offered and boards can be rented at the quieter south end of the beach.

FRESHWATER BEACH, MANLY, NEAR SYDNEY, AUSTRALIA—Right next door to bustling Manly, Freshwater Beach (or Freshie), one of Sydney's northern beaches, is friendly and unpretentious. Freshwater is popular with longboarders, making it a mellow place to learn to surf.

JACO BEACH, COSTA RICA—Jaco Beach has a small beach break with left and right peaks that are fun, and you can surf almost the entire beach. It tends to close out when the waves are over head high and during low tide. Jaco Beach is a popular jump-off point for surfers traveling to Costa Rica because it is only about a two-hour drive from San José. You can get off the plane and surf the same day!

KUTA BEACH, BALI—This is the ideal beach for testing your surfing skills. For surfing equipment, head for the dozen or so local surf shops. Run by veteran surfers, these shops rent and sell surfboards, boogie boards, accessories, and tide charts. These guys can also give you current information on the state of the surf. Surfboards can be rented on the beach.

NGARUNUI BEACH, RAGLAN, NEW ZEALAND—Located on the west coast of New Zealand, Raglan Town's (Rag Town's) Ngarunui Beach is a sandy beach, which is great for beginner-to-intermediate surfers. The beach has lifeguard coverage throughout the season. The local surf school has an equipment trailer that is parked on the beach during the spring and summer season. It has an assortment of surfboards and wet suits for rent, or you can sign up to take a lesson.

PLAYA ACAPULQUITO, SAN JOSÉ DEL CABO, BAJA, MEXICO—Stay at the Cabo Surf Hotel, which fronts the beach, or stop by for the day and rent boards and/or get a lesson. Playa Acapulquito is not crowded and it offers long rides. The spot is a favorite of surfers from around the globe.

PLAYA DE GROS, SAN SEBASTIAN, SPAIN—Playa de Gros has a nice mellow longboard wave, but it can get very crowded. This spot breaks over a sand bottom, so it's not particularly dangerous.

PLAYA JOBOS, PUERTO RICO—Playa Jobos is a popular beach with swimmers and surfers. There is a smooth sandbar inside this cove that creates pleasant beginner waves. Surf shops nearby will rent you a board, and there is a local surf school.

PLAYA PRINCIPAL, PICHILEMU, CHILE—The beaches of Pichilemu are recognized not only for their beauty and tranquillity but also for their excellent conditions of wind and surf. There is a great left break on the principal beach of Pichilemu with an inner set of much smaller waves that are great for beginners. There are rentals and lessons at the local surf shop or multiday lesson packages that include cabanas and meals.

RIBEIRA D'ILHAS, ERICEIRA, PORTUGAL—Ericeira is a famous surfing town just north of Lisbon. Ribeira D'Ilhas is the ideal surf break: it's situated inside a bay, so it has less wind than some of the neighboring breaks. There are plenty of parking and local surf shops in town to rent you a board.

SAYULITA, NAYARIT, MEXICO—Just twenty-two miles north of Puerto Vallarta, Sayulita is a picturesque fishing village that offers great beginner surf. The all-girl surf school and camp Las Olas calls Sayulita home. During the summer months, almost the entire coast of Nayarit can be a surfer's haven. From the **San Blas** area all the way south into **Banderas Bay,** there's a whole list of great surfing breaks.

SURFERS CORNER, MUIZENBERG, CAPE TOWN, SOUTH AFRICA—Surfers Corner has a great friendly wave for beginners, and it is also popular with longboarders. There is a surf school located on Beach Road, where you can take a lesson or rent a board.

TAITO BEACH, CHIBA, JAPAN—Located about an hour southeast of Tokyo, the region of Chiba is known for surf. Taito has strictly a longboard wave, and it is a very safe place for all levels of surfers. Be wary of the ropes that hold down old tires and sandbags to keep the sandbar in place.

TOFINO, VANCOUVER ISLAND, BRITISH COLUMBIA—Located on the west coast of Vancouver Island, Tofino's spectacular beaches are some of the most pristine in the world, and they are surrounded by a majestic temperate rain forest. Quite a few schools and surf shops offer lessons, so finding someone to take you out or rent you a board should be easy. Getting into the chilly water, however, might be more difficult.

TUNCUNS, BUZIOS, BRAZIL—Buzios is located 110 miles from the town of Rio, in the state of Rio de Janeiro. A former peaceful fishing village, the town and its peninsula, dotted with twenty-three sandy beaches, has turned into an artist colony and a favorite seaside retreat for Rio's trendy people and travelers from all over the world. It is also a surfing paradise, with perfect conditions for surfing, windsurfing, and kite surfing. A surf school is located right on Tuncuns beach, one of the best surf spots in the area, and they will rent you boards or give you lessons.

Badass Breaks

It's fun to know the names of some of the most well-known surf breaks on the planet. Here are some names of places where you have *no* business paddling out. Lookie, no touchie:

DUNGEONS, CAPE TOWN, SOUTH AFRICA—Dungeons is often thought of as the Maverick's of South Africa because the waves only break here in winter months. The water temps, therefore, are usually in the low 50s. Brrr! Oh yeah, and there are sharks. For the brave few that choose to ride Dungeons, waves can be found here that are up to 40 feet tall.

JAWS, MAUI, HAWAII—Jaws (also known as Peahi, Hawaiian for "beckon") doesn't even begin to break until it is 12 feet. It doesn't become a formed wave until it's about 20 feet, and it has been known to see 80-foot faces. Yikes! Tow-in surfers like Laird Hamilton, using personal watercrafts and specialized surfboards, have seemingly tamed Jaws, but even they respect the awesome power that produces these waves.

KILLER'S, ISLA TODOS SANTOS, BAJA, MEXICO—This legendary world-class big-wave break is located on Todos Santos Island, twelve miles off Ensenada, Baja, near an offshore canyon on the northwest tip of the island, in front of the lighthouse. The waves are typically two to four times bigger here than when they reach the shore in Baja. Faces of more than 60 feet have been known to march in at Killer's.

MAVERICK'S, HALF MOON BAY, CALIFORNIA—Named after a German shepherd that followed a group of surfers into the water in 1961, Maverick's is located just off the Half Moon Bay harbor south of San Francisco and can handle waves as big as 40 or 50 feet. These waves are ridden now by tow-in surfers, but paddle-in surfers always have the right of way. Seems insane in either case, especially since the water temperature usually hovers around 50 degrees. Only a few women have challenged it. Sarah Gerhardt was the first—you go, girl!

PIPELINE, OAHU, HAWAII—Surfers didn't even think it was rideable until the 1960s. Now Pipeline is the world's premier surf spot. During a big swell, the waves get progressively bigger the farther one goes out, but it is on the ridiculously shallow First Reef, located less than 50 yards offshore, where the waves are the most hollow and drain the water off the reef in a single horrifying slurp, making wipeouts into only inches of water a total bitch. (Other top North Shore spots include **Sunset Beach** and **Waimea Bay**.)

PUERTO ESCONDIDO, OAXACA, MEXICO—Known as the Mexican Pipeline, Puerto Escondido waves are funneled through an underwater canyon and break in huge, mean barrels onto a sandy bottom. Waves can range anywhere from 4 to 15 feet, and the area boasts radical currents and deadly riptides. During a contest in the early 1980s, a fledgling Mexican pro drifted from view during his heat and was never seen again.

TEAHUPOO, TAHITI, FRENCH POLYNESIA—Teahupoo (pronounced "Te-a-hu-po-o" by the locals and "cho-pu" by Westerners) is known as the heaviest wave in the world. The reef lies about a third of a mile off the shores of Tahiti, and beyond the reef the bottom drops abruptly to more than 300 feet. Large south swells generated off New Zealand slam into the reef, unchallenged by a continental shelf, causing the wave to thicken rather than push upward and producing a lip as thick as its height.

Epilogue

I GET IT IN MY HEAD that I will take the next wave in. I've been surfing for a couple of hours, and I am tired and thirsty. I look to the horizon and it's totally flat. Nada. Nothing. No waves.

I can't paddle in (that would break some weird surfer's code I have internalized). I'm probably getting a parking ticket even as we speak.

That's the thing about surfing: it's so much fun, it's so addicting, and it puts everything else into perspective. It makes trivial things seem, well, trivial.

I encourage you to become a surfer girl. The only way to learn how to surf is to surf! So get out there; go as often as you can. Don't be scared. It is difficult—and don't let anyone tell you differently. It will take you a long time to get decent and even longer to become good. Boys will lie and tell you it only took them a couple of times before they were shredding—not so. It takes months and, depending on how often you go, even years. As a friend of mine says, it's a wave ratio. Number of waves ridden equals how much you improve. So you have to get out there and catch at least a hundred waves before you can even think about doing a cutback or hanging ten. But it's worth it. It is *so* worth it.

I see a wave on the horizon. I paddle hard toward it, then swing around and point my nose toward shore. It picks me up and I ride it in. But you know what? It wasn't my best ride. Maybe I'll paddle out for just one more.

Glossary

Aerial When you launch your board off the wave into the air (oh yeah, and you've got to land it).

Backside Surfing with your back to the wave.

Bail Fall off your board on purpose (usually before a large wave threatens to kick your butt).

Barrel (also **tube)** The inside of a hollow wave.

Beach break A surf location where waves break all along on a sandy beach.

Blank A block of foam from which a surfboard is shaped.

Blown out Choppy surf resulting from onshore winds (this makes for crappy surf conditions).

Bottom turn A maneuver at the bottom of the wave face that brings you back into the sweet spot on the wave.

Break Surf location; also when the wave steepens and spills over into white water.

Carving Making turns along the face of the wave.

Channel Deep-water sections between sandbanks or reefs.

Choppy Rough, irregular waves.

Clean Glassy, peeling waves; also good surf conditions.

Cleanup A large wave or set that catches everybody on the shore side of the breaking wave (results in total mayhem).

Closeout A wave that breaks along its entire length simultaneously, leaving you with no place to take off.

Crest Top or lip of the wave or swell.

Cross step Proper form when walking a longboard, with one foot crossing over the other—as opposed to "shuffling."

Curl Concave face of the wave just ahead of the barrel (as in the 1960s expression "shoot the curl!").

Cutback An S-turn on the face of the wave that takes you back into the sweet spot or pocket just ahead of the white water if you have gotten too far ahead of it.

Dawn patrol Early-morning surf session.

Deck Top of a surfboard.

Ding A dent, crack, or hole on the surfboard (bummer).

Dropping in Taking off on a wave

when someone who is nearer to the peak is already up and riding (this is very, very bad etiquette).

Duck dive Pushing your board and yourself under a wave when paddling out.

Face The unbroken surface of the front of a wave.

Fin (also **skeg)** Rudder devices on the bottom rear of the board that are used for balance and control. Can be single fin, double fin, or trifin (three are the most stable; one is the most maneuverable).

Flat No waves at all, unsurfable.

Floater Floating your board on the falling part of the wave, then dropping down with the white water and landing it.

Getting tubed Surfing inside the barrel of a hollow wave and getting spit out.

Getting worked Getting thrown off your board and thrashed around underwater by the surf (this is really, really fun—just kidding).

Glass off When the wind dies down, which causes the conditions to become smooth.

Glassy When the ocean is smooth as a result of calm wind conditions.

Gnarly Awesome; also big, mean waves.

Goofy foot A surfer who surfs with her right foot forward on the board.

Grommet or **grom** Young surfer.

Groundswell Swell from a distant storm.

Gun A big-wave board, long and narrow in shape.

Hang five To ride with five toes curled over the nose of a longboard.

Hang ten (also **toes to the nose)** Standing on a longboard with both your feet on the nose.

Haole Hawaiian term for a Caucasian.

Home break Location you mainly surf.

Impact zone The point when a wave is breaking most frequently and heavily.

Inside Shore side of a wave.

Kick out Ending your ride by going up and over the top of the wave toward the horizon.

Kook Someone who thinks he knows how to surf but doesn't.

Leash Cord that attaches the board to the surfer's ankle or knee.

Left A wave that breaks from right to left from the rider's point of view.

Lineup The place you sit and wait to ride a wave.

Lip The part of the wave that pitches out as the wave is breaking.

Local Someone surfing her home break.

Lull Pause between sets of waves.

Malibu Surf town in Southern California; also name for a longboard for those outside the United States (also **Minimal**).

Mushy Slow, sloppy wave with little power.

Namaste Often used at the end of yoga practice, the word *namaste* is an ancient Sanskrit blessing done while placing the hands together at the heart, closing the eyes, and bowing the head. It means, "I bow to the divine spark in you."

Noodle arms (also **spaghetti arms)** When your arms have no strength left in them and become as limp as noodles (usually after hours of surfing).

Nose The front of the board.

Nose guard A piece of rubber that goes over the nose of a pointy board to protect you from more intense pain when you get hit.

Nose riding Technique used by longboarders who ride with one or two feet on nose of the board.

Offshore Winds that blow from land to the ocean (good for surfing).

Off-the-lip Maneuver where the board hits the breaking lip of the wave before continuing along the face.

Onshore Winds that blow from the ocean onto land (bad for surfing).

Outside Horizon side of a breaking wave or set.

Over-the-falls A wipeout where you fall with the curtain of the wave and get pushed underwater by the lip (yeah, this sucks).

Peak The point where the wave breaks first, from which it ideally peels in one or both directions.

Pearl To wipe out when the nose of the board buries itself under water and the back flips up and throws you off.

Peel A wave that breaks cleanly and evenly from the peak.

Pocket The steepest and most powerful part of the wave, just ahead and under the breaking lip.

Point break A surf location around a point of land where the waves break consistently in the same spot and peel out in one direction.

Pop-up Method of getting to your feet from a prone position on your board.

Pumping (also **going off** or **firing)** Term used to describe a good, powerful swell.

Pumping the board A means of increasing speed across the face of a wave by slightly bouncing the board.

Quiver A selection of surfboards for different conditions.

Rail The sides or edges of a board.

Reef break Waves breaking over a rising from the seabed—usually a coral reef or rock shelf.

Regular foot A surfer who surfs with his left foot forward.

Resin Chemical used in a two-part mixture with a catalyst to convert fiberglass into a hard outer skin of a surfboard.

Right A wave that breaks from left to right from the rider's point of view.

Rip, ripping, ripper Awesome surfing, awesome surfer.

Rocker The curve in a surfboard when viewed from its side.

Sandbank A bank of elevated sand on which waves break.

Set A group of waves.

Shaper Someone who makes surfboards.

Shore break Waves that break right on the beach; usually not surfable.

Shoulder The unbroken face of a wave ahead of the white water.

Slater Kelly Slater, winner of six world titles (and incredibly hot to boot!).

Snake To continually paddle around someone in order to get into a better spot to catch a wave (considered bad etiquette).

Soul surfer Usually associated with a longboarder who surfs with the waves without trying to perform any radical maneuvers; also a talented surfer who doesn't compete.

Soup The white water of a broken wave.

Spongers Surfers' affectionate (not really) nickname for bodyboarders.

Stick Surfboard.

Stringer The thin piece of wood running down the center of a board from nose to tail.

Surf stoke Unable to stop thinking about surfing.

Surf's up Dated expression meaning surfing conditions are good.

Sweet spot The unbroken section of wave directly in front of the white water.

Swell Wind-generated waves from varying distances.

Switch-foot A surfer who can surf with either foot forward.

Tail The rear end of the board.

Takeoff The start of a ride.

Tandem Two people surfing on a board and performing tricks together.

Three-sixty Spinning the board 360 degrees on the face of the wave or in the air (and, of course, landing it).

Thruster A tri-finned surfboard.

Tow-in surfing Using a personal watercraft (jet ski), surfers are pulled into a wave by a tow rope to reach speeds needed to surf big waves.

Trimming Adjusting weight and position on the board so that the board retains maximum speed.

Trough The lowest area of the wave as it begins to break; also the low part of the wave between unbroken wave sets.

Tube See barrel.

Turtle roll Not sushi. Used with a longboard during the paddle out. As the white water approaches, you roll over onto your back, taking your board with you and letting the wave pass over you (abroad it's known as an **Eskimo roll**).

Wahine Hawaiian word for female; also a surfer girl.

Waterwoman A woman skilled in all aspects of the ocean.

Weekend warrior Someone who works or goes to school full-time and can only surf on the weekends.

Wind swell A weak swell generated by localized winds.

Wipeout Falling off your board hard (usually involves massive amounts of water going up your nose).

Resources

Surf Schools

There are plenty of good surf schools out there. Check on the Internet under "surf school" and include the name of your area. The following is a list of some all-female surf schools and camps around the world where you can get your surf on in a noncompetitive atmosphere.

The Betty Series
P.O. BOX 510815
MELBOURNE BEACH, FLORIDA 32951
321-455-2297
WWW.THEBETTYSERIES.COM

The name Betty is actually an inside joke. It refers to girls, called Bettys back in the 1960s, who would just sit on the beach and watch the boys surf. Missy Sixberry, her sister, and her mother decided to start their own extreme sports camps for girls who don't want to just sit on the sidelines anymore. Women or girls who wish to learn and compete in sports such as surfing, wakeboarding, skateboarding, or snowboarding can look to the Bettys for help. The Betty Surf Camp is held daily from 9:00 A.M. to 3:00 P.M. Weekend clinics are also available in Cocoa Beach and Galvaston, Texas.

Big Island Girl Surf
P.O. BOX 10452
HILO, HAWAII 96721
808-326-0269
WWW.BIGISLANDGIRLSURF.COM

B.I.G. Surf is located on the Hilo side of the Big Island of Hawaii. It offers overnight surf adventure camps for girls and women as well as mother (auntie)/daughter weeks. The weeklong overnight camps cater to everyone, from beginners to advanced surfers, and include accommodations, tasty healthy meals, yoga/stretch classes, surf lessons, local activities, and excursions that may include snorkeling with dolphins, camping, hula dancing, and/or tropical rain forest hikes.

Kelea Surf Spa

NORTH SHORE, OAHU *OR*
MALPAIS, COSTA RICA
949-492-7263
WWW.KELEASURFSPA.COM

*Named after Kelea, the ancient Hawaiian chieftess who gave
up her position to live by the ocean so she could surf, Kelea
lures women away from their stressful lives into an environment
where the greatest worry is sand in your surf wax. Packages include
five-night/six-day accommodations, three meals a day, surf lessons,
yoga classes, hiking, and massage. A typical day includes a tropical breakfast;
surf lessons; gourmet lunch; either yoga, power walking, snorkeling, or hiking followed by body
treatments, including massage and/or facials; and then dinner.*

Las Olas Surf Safaris for Women

991 TYLER STREET, SUITE 101
BENICIA, CALIFORNIA 94510
707-746-6435
WWW.SURFLASOLAS.COM

*Las Olas Surf Safari's goal is to be a reverse finishing school. Las Olas
creates a unique experience born from the understanding that women
attain confidence, health, friendship, and fun by enjoying sports together.
Since 1997, their all-female safaris have offered women the chance to learn
surfing in a no-pressure, nonjudgmental, warm-water environment. One-week camps
are held in Sayulita, Mexico, just one hour from Puerto Vallarta.*

Maui Surfer Girls

P.O. BOX 1158
PUUNENE, HAWAII 96784
808-280-8165
WWW.MAUISURFERGIRLS.COM

*Maui Surfer Girls is a school and camp for teenage girls on the
west shore of Maui in Oluwalu. Its mission is to provide
adolescent girls with a safe and fun environment in which to gain
technical skills and self-confidence through surfing. It provides
quality surf instruction and mentorship, promotes self-esteem, and
provides campers with an unforgettable experience. In addition to surfing
lessons, a luau, beach party, bonfires, adventure trips, and craft projects expose campers to the
Hawaiian culture. There is also a seven-day all-inclusive mother/daughter retreat. Look for
international trips to Brazil, New Zealand, and Indonesia. Maui Surfer Girls offers day, weekend,
and two-week surf camps for girls aged twelve to seventeen.*

Nancy Emerson School of Surfing
358 PAPA PLACE, SUITE F
KAHULUI, MAUI 96732
808-244-7873
WWW.SURFCLINICS.COM

Nancy Emerson, international professional surfing champion, is the originator of the world famous "Learn to Surf in One Lesson" technique. Nancy Emerson School of Surfing focuses on the complete surfing experience: water safety, ocean awareness, and wave conditions. Its instructors coach with a keen eye to the subtle aspects of form. They help not only the beginner, but also the experienced and professional surfer as well. All instructors are personally trained and certified by Nancy. Clinics are also held on the Gold Coast of Australia and in Malibu, California.

Pura Vida Adventures
MALPAIS, COSTA RICA
415-465-2162
WWW.PURAVIDAADVENTURES.COM

Pura vida to a Costa Rican means "life is great." Pura Vida Adventures is about giving women the opportunity to learn or improve their surfing skills in a fun and noncompetitive environment. And surfing is just part of the adventure. Yoga, massage, breathtaking sunsets, and exposure to new cultures would all be part of your experience. Pura Vida offers one-week surf adventures in Costa Rica.

Surf Academy
811 N. CATALINA AVENUE, #2316
REDONDO BEACH, CALIFORNIA 90277
877-599-7873
WWW.SURFACADEMY.COM

Surf Academy will take your surfing skills to the next level with a coed staff of certified surf instructors. The average is one instructor to four or five students. Surf Academy's classes are offered at three locations: El Segundo, Santa Monica, and Huntington Beach. Each Saturday is Women's Surfday: a two-hour lesson for all girls and women ages seven and up. And in the summertime, there are weeklong day camps for girls ages eight through sixteen. Private lessons are available as well.

Surf Diva
LA JOLLA SHORES
SAN DIEGO, CALIFORNIA
858-454-8273
WWW.SURFDIVA.COM

Surf Diva offers a fun and active two-day course for beginner and intermediate surfers at La Jolla Shores in San Diego. Learn ocean awareness, priority rules, paddling, and wave riding. This is a great introductory course to get your feet wet! Clinics are offered every weekend (two hours on Saturday and two hours on Sunday).

Surf Sister Surf School

BOX 6
TOFINO, BRITISH COLUMBIA, CANADA
V0R 2Z0
1-877-724-7873
WWW.SURFSISTER.COM

Canada's only all-women's surf school began in Tofino, British Columbia, in 1999, and was founded by Jenny Stewart, longtime Tofino surfer and Canadian women's surfing champion. Its goal is to promote women's surfing not only in Tofino but also worldwide. Surf Sister introduces women of all ages and abilities to the sport of surfing in a safe, fun, and supportive environment. Daily classes and weekend clinics are available.

SwellWomen

P.O. BOX 1294
PUUNENE, HAWAII 96784
WWW.SWELLWOMEN.COM
1-800-399-6284

SwellWomen is a seven-night/eight-day surf-and-yoga experience on the beautiful island of Maui for women aged eighteen and older. High-quality staff, healthy and delicious food, surf and yoga instruction, and other wellness programs are available. It also provides afternoon excursions exploring the rain forest or snorkeling in some secret spots on the west side of the island.

U.S. Surf Magazines

What do you do when the conditions are flat or you are miles from the ocean? Pick up one of these great surf mags and check out breaks you will someday surf or the pros you may someday beat!

FOR WOMEN

SG (Surf, Snow, Skate Girl): www.sgmag.com
Surf Life for Women: www.surflifeforwomen.com

OTHERS

Longboard Magazine: www.longboardmagazine.com
Surfer: www.surfermag.com
Surfer's Journal: www.surfersjournal.com
Surfing: www.surfingthemag.com
Transworld Surf: www.transworldsurf.com
Water Magazine: www.waterzine.com

Film

Here are some surf films that actually made it into a theater. Good or bad, the following films have shaped America's view of the surfer. Check them out on a stormy day; some will inspire you and some are good for a chuckle.

Riding Giants (directed by Stacy Peralta, Sony Pictures Classics, 2004)
Step into Liquid (directed by Dana Brown, Artisan, August 2003)
Blue Crush (directed by John Stockwell, Universal Studios, August 2002)
In God's Hands (directed by Zalman King, Tristar, 1998)
Point Break (directed by Kathryn Bigelow, 20th Century Fox, 1991)
North Shore (directed by William Phelps, Universal Pictures, 1987)
Big Wednesday (directed by John Milius, Warner Brothers, 1978)
Endless Summer (directed by Bruce Brown, Bruce Brown Films, 1966)
Ride the Wild Surf (directed by Don Taylor, Columbia Pictures, 1964)
Beach Party (directed by William Asher, AIP, 1963)
Gidget (directed by Paul Wendkos, Columbia Pictures, 1959)

Video

There are lots of surf videos out there showcasing surfers ripping it up to bitchin' sound tracks in beautiful locations. You can pick one up at your local surf shop or purchase it online (occasionally your video store may carry them, but they are hard to find for rent). The all-female videos listed below show your favorite professional female surfers rocking, ripping, and shredding.

AKA: GIRL SURFER (Whyte House, 2004). A 16-mm documentary that follows the compelling personal and professional journeys of six of the world's most talented female surfers.

BLUE CRUSH (surf video; Billygoat Productions, 1998). Lisa Andersen, Rochelle Ballard, Layne Beachley, Serena Brooke, Megan Abubo, Trudy Todd, Keala Kennelly, Pauline Menczer, Prue Jeffries, and Sophia Mulanovich surf exotic locations.

A GIRL'S SURF ADDICTION (O'Neill USA, SG Magazine, and Sky Rondenet Films, 2004). Features Rochelle Ballard and Melanie Bartels surfing with their friends and having fun at world-class surf breaks.

MODUS MIX (Billygoat Productions, 2003). Rochelle Ballard, Keala Kennelly, Layne Beachley, Lisa Andersen, Megan Abubo, Serena Brooke, Kate Skarratt, Chelsea Georgeson, Sophia Mulanovich, Sam Cornish, and Holly Beck surf the globe.

PEACHES (Billygoat Productions, 2000). Features Keala Kennelly, Layne Beachley, and Rochelle Ballard.

POETIC SILENCE (Billygoat Productions, 2003). Set in the Metawai Islands, this video stars Rochelle Ballard, Megan Abubo, Serena Brooke, and friends.

7 GIRLS (Roxy/XX Productions, 2001). Adventure around the globe with Layne Beachley, Serena Brooke, Heather Clark, Megan Abubo, Rochelle Ballard, Keala Kennelly, and Sophia Mulanovich.

THE SURFER'S JOURNAL BIOGRAPHIES: GREATS OF WOMEN'S SURFING (Surfer's Journal, 2002). Great female surfing legends and their impact on the history of surfing.

TROPICAL MADNESS (Jet Girl Films, 2001). Gives a taste of pro surfers' lives on the World Tour.

And check out these how-to videos:

ROXY: LEARN TO SURF, NOW (Roxy and Blue Field Entertainment, 2002). Learn to surf with team rider Kassia Meador and friends.

YOGA FOR SURFERS (Volume I: *Yoga for Surfers* and Volume II: *Fluid Power Yoga for Surfers*). Peggy Hall, along with surfers Rochelle Ballard and Taylor Knox, guides you through a yoga workout designed specifically for surfers.

Web Sites

There are tons of Web sites that feature surfing. Type in "surfing girls" in your Web browser and you will get a listing of over a million sites. Here are some of my favorites to get you started on your path to being a surfing superstar!

GO PRO

www.aspworldtour.com—Site for Association Surfing Professionals, with information on top surfers and major contests.

www.nssa.org—The NSSA is the highest-profile amateur competitive surfing association in the United States. With a special emphasis on student surfers, the NSSA membership is open to anyone who wants to surf competitively as an amateur.

www.wilsurfing.com—Women's International Longboarding site.

www.womenssurfing.org—International Women's Surfing site dedicated to female professional surfers.

FIND YOUR GEAR

www.beckersurf.com—Loads of surf brands are carried at Becker.

www.billabonggirls.com—Billabong's site for the ladies.

www.bodyglove.com—Body Glove's clothing and surf equipment.

www.etniesgirl.com—Check out Etnies' clothing and tennies for the ladies as well as team riders and extras.

www.hurley.com—Hurley site for surfer girl clothing and swimwear.

www.indoboard.com—Get your balance boards here!

www.oneill.com—O'Neill's clothing and surf gear site.

www.ripcurlgirl.com—Rip Curl's site for girls' fashion.

www.roxy.com—Roxy clothing line, and information on contests and team riders.

www.surf-chick.com—Real clothes for real surfer girls.

www.swell.com—Everything you would ever want to buy for surfing.

FIND EVERYTHING

www.boardfolio.com—Links you to all kinds of surf sites.

www.isurfing.com—Surfer's directory with links to surf-related pages.

INFO

www.eastcoastwahines.com—News and contest info for East Coast female surfers.

www.sistersofthesea.com—Female surfers out of Jacksonville, Florida, who love to surf and organize surf contests and cleanup days.

www.surfhistory.com—Includes a history of the sport as well as features on surfing legends.

www.wahinesurfing.com—International female surfing zine.

SURF REPORTS

www.buoyweather.com—For buoy data around the world.

www.stormsurf.com—Buoy data and surf reports around the world.

www.surfline.com—News, links, and surf reports.

www.surflink.com—A division of the Action Sports Network with surf reports and video of your favorite surf spot.

www.surfrider.org—Features beach-quality reports and closures.

www.wannasurf.com—Surf spots around the world, created by surfers for surfers.

From your Verizon cell phone, call *SURF for an automated Surfline report of your local spot (fifty cents per call).

Philanthropies

Give back.

BOARDING FOR BREAST CANCER (www.b4bc.org). Boarding for Breast Cancer is a nonprofit, youth-focused education, awareness, and fund-raising foundation. Its mission is to increase awareness about breast cancer, the importance of early detection, and the value of a healthy lifestyle.

GREENPEACE (www.greenpeace.org). As a global organization, Greenpeace focuses on the most crucial worldwide threats to our planet's biodiversity and environment. Members campaign to stop climate change, protect ancient forests, save the oceans, stop whaling, say no to genetic engineering, stop the nuclear threat, eliminate toxic chemicals, and encourage sustainable trade.

HEAL THE BAY (www.healthebay.org). Heal the Bay is a nonprofit environmental organization dedicated to making Santa Monica Bay and Southern California coastal waters safe and healthy for people and marine life. It uses research, education, community action, and policy programs to achieve this goal.

LIFE ROLLS ON (www.liferollson.com). Life Rolls On (LRO) is a nonprofit foundation dedicated to increasing awareness about spinal cord injuries within the youth culture through the influential action of sports figures.

OCEANA (www.oceana.org). Oceana campaigns to protect and restore the world's oceans. Its teams of marine scientists, economists, lawyers, and advocates win specific and concrete policy changes to reduce pollution and to prevent the irreversible collapse of fish populations, marine mammals, and other sea life.

THE OCEAN CONSERVANCY (www.oceanconservancy.org). Through science-based advocacy, research, and public education, The Ocean Conservancy informs, inspires, and empowers people to speak and act for the oceans.

SURF AID INTERNATIONAL (www.surfaidinternational.org). Surf Aid International encourages fund-raising from the international surfing community to achieve measurable and sustainable improvements in the health of the Mentawai people by implementing health projects.

SURFRIDER FOUNDATION (www.surfrider.org). The Surfrider Foundation is a nonprofit environmental organization dedicated to the protection and enjoyment of the world's oceans, waves, and beaches for all people through conservation, activism, research, and education.

WORLD WILDLIFE FOUNDATION (www.wwf.org). WWF's mission is to stop the degradation of the planet's natural environment and to build a future in which humans live in harmony with nature.

Bibliography

Books

Burrow, Taj. *Taj Burrow's Book of Hot Surfing.* California: Wilderness Press, 2004.

Gabbard, Andrea. *Girl in the Curl: A Century of Women in Surfing.* Seattle: Seal Press, 2000.

Kampion, Drew. *The Book of Waves.* Colorado: Roberts Rinehart Publishers, 1997.

Snyder, Rocky. *Fit to Surf: A Surfer's Guide to Strength and Conditioning.* Ohio: International Marine/Ragged Mountain Press, 2003.

Warshaw, Matt. *The Encyclopedia of Surfing.* Florida: Harcourt, 2003.

Werner, Doug. *Surfer's Start-Up: A Beginner's Guide to Surfing* (Start-Up Sports Series). California: Tracks Publishing, 1999.

Magazine Articles

Aromando, Lorraine. "Hanging 20, Surfing and Pregnancy." *Surf Life for Women.* Summer 2004, Issue #9.

Barilotti, Steve. "PSI, The Ten Most Powerful Breaks in the World." *Surfer Magazine.* September 2002, Volume 43, Issue #9.

Hall, Peggy. "Cross Training." *Surf Life for Women.* Fall 2003, Issue #6.

Web Articles

Gault-Williams, Malcolm. "Legendary Women Surfers of the Wooden Era." *Legendary Surfers*, vol. 2, chap. 20. http://www. legendarysurfers.com

Greer, David. "How to Treat Sunburn." *Pagewise*, 2002. http://wy. essortment.com/howtreatsunbur_rfdh.htm

Marcus, Ben. "From Polynesia, with Love: The History of Surfing from Captain Cook to the Present." *Surfing for Life*. http://www. surfingforlife.com/history.html

Tackett, Chad. "Benefits of Flexibility Training." *Personal Health Zone*. http://www.personalhealthzone.com/flex.html

Yronwode, Catherine. "Saint Christopher, Patron of Safe Travel," *The Lucky W Amulet Archive*. http://www.luckymojo.com/saintchristopher.html

"The History of Surfing: Women Surfers." SurfArt.com. http://www. surfart.com/surf_history/women.html

"Jellyfish, Stingray and other Water Animal, Bites/Stings." *Emedicinehealth*. http://www.emedicinehealth.com/collections/CO1608.asp

"Substance Reports: The Sun and Sunscreens," ivillage. http://beauty. ivillage.com/skin/sreports/article/0,,230119,00.html

"Surfing A–Z." and "Surf Glossary." *Surfline*. http://www.surfline.com/surfology/surfology_a2z_index.cfm

"Tan Me!" Health and Beauty, *Good Housekeeping*. http://magazines. ivillage.com/goodhousekeeping/hb/health/articles/0,,284598_ 428995,00.html?arrivalSA=1&cobrandRef=0&arrival_freqCap=2

"Water Safety Tips." American Red Cross. http://www.redcross.org/ services/hss/tips/healthtips/safetywater.html#beach

Acknowledgments

ALOHA NUI LOA TO:

My mom, dad, and especially Debra.

My surf sisters: Dana, Jessica, Maria, Marissa, Rachael, Robbie, and Shelly.

My surf brothers: Adam, Barlo, Johnny, Jose, Ogle, and Werley.

Julie Barer, Natalie Kaire, and Sujean Rim for their brilliance and enthusiasm. Rochelle Ballard for her kick-ass Foreword and her tireless contributions to women's surfing.

The experts: George Burgess (sharks), Nick Fash (marine life), Peggy Hall (yoga and nutrition), Dr. Mary Kerr (ob/gyn), Dr. Peter Koh (eyes), Dr. Raphael Nach (ears), Eileen Stein (nutrition), and Dr. Heather Roberts (skin).

Many thanks to the countless surfers around the world for their help and generosity in sharing their surf spots with me.